Ugetsu

Rutgers Films in Print

Charles Affron, Mirella Jona Affron, and Robert Lyons, editors

My Darling Clementine, John Ford, director
edited by Robert Lyons

The Last Metro, François Truffaut, director
edited by Mirella Jona Affron and E. Rubinstein

Touch of Evil, Orson Welles, director
edited by Terry Comito

The Marriage of Maria Braun, Rainer Werner Fassbinder, director
edited by Joyce Rheuban

Letter from an Unknown Woman, Max Ophuls, director
edited by Virginia Wright Wexman with Karen Hollinger

Rashomon, Akira Kurosawa, director
edited by Donald Richie

8½, Federico Fellini, director
edited by Charles Affron

La Strada, Federico Fellini, director
edited by Peter Bondanella and Manuela Gieri

Breathless, Jean-Luc Godard, director
edited by Dudley Andrew

Bringing Up Baby, Howard Hawks, director
edited by Gerald Mast

Chimes at Midnight, Orson Welles, director
edited by Bridget Gellert Lyons

L'avventura, Michelangelo Antonioni, director
edited by Seymour Chatman and Guido Fink

Meet John Doe, Frank Capra, director
edited by Charles Wolfe

Invasion of the Body Snatchers, Don Siegel, director
edited by Al LaValley

Memories of Underdevelopment, Tomás Gutiérrez Alea, director
introduction by Michael Chanan

Imitation of Life, Douglas Sirk, director
edited by Lucy Fischer

Ugetsu, Kenji Mizoguchi, director
edited by Keiko I. McDonald

Ugetsu

Kenji Mizoguchi,

director

Keiko I. McDonald, editor

Rutgers University Press

New Brunswick, New Jersey

Ugetsu is volume 17 in the Rutgers
Films in Print Series
Copyright © 1993 by Rutgers, The State University
Manufactured in the United States of America

Library of Congress Cataloging-in-Publication Data
Ugetsu: Kenji Mizoguchi, director / Keiko I.
  McDonald, editor.
     p.   cm.—(Rutgers films in print; v. 17)
     Filmography: p.
     Includes bibliographical references (p.   ).
     ISBN 0-8135-1861-X (cloth)
     ISBN 0-8135-1862-8 (pbk.)
     1. Ugetsu monogatari (Motion picture).
I. Mizoguchi, Kenji, 1898–1956. II. McDonald,
Keiko I. III. Ugetsu monogatari (Motion
picture) IV. Series.
PN1997.U373U34   1992
791.43'72—dc20   92-8419
                                 CIP

British Cataloging-in-Publication information available

Acknowledgments

This project could never have been completed without the generous assistance of a number of people.

I would like to express my most sincere gratitude to Donald Richie, who unselfishly shared with me his expertise in Japanese cinema.

I am particularly grateful to the following leading film critics of Japan who generously allowed me to translate their publications into English: Tadao Sato, Ichiro Ueno, and the late Yoshikata Yoda.

I would also like to thank Joanne Bernardi for allowing me to consult her thesis on Yoshikata Yoda's original *Ugetsu* script, which includes a translation of the script itself.

I also owe a great debt of gratitude to Charles and Mirella Affron, David G. Anderson, Linda Ehrlich, Robert Lyons, David Mills, and Dana Polan, on whose linguistic competence I relied very heavily.

Special thanks are due Thomas Rouse, who offered technical assistance in completing the continuity text.

I am indebted to the general editors for this series, especially Robert Lyons, who went over my continuity text and essays thoroughly and offered valuable suggestions.

I would also like to thank Leslie Mitchner, Executive Editor at Rutgers University Press, for continuous encouragement.

Akira Shimizu and Kanako Hayashi from the Kawakita Film Institute/the Japan Film Library Council, and Masatoshi Oba from Film Center of the Tokyo National Museum of Art were wonderfully accommodating in providing access to the libraries of their facilities.

Research work for this book, including a trip to Japan in the summer of 1988, was supported by the Japan Foundation, the Toshiba International Foundation, and the Japan Iron and Steel Federation Endowment Funds of the University of Pittsburgh. I owe special thanks to these organizations.

Contents

Introduction

Ugetsu:
Why Is It a
Masterpiece?

Keiko I. McDonald

K enji Mizoguchi's *Ugetsu Monogatari* (*Ugetsu*, 1953), like Akira Kurosawa's *Rashomon* (1951), is one of the few Japanese films that has gained
international renown. The positive response to it, however, was not immediate. In Japan, at the time of its release, the film attracted little attention. Just the
year before, Mizoguchi's *Saikaku Ichidai Ohna* (*The Life of Oharu*) was greeted
as a masterpiece by critics indifferent to *Ugetsu*. Among the few critics who were
favorably disposed was Ichiro Ueno. Ueno did recognize the importance of the
film's thematic material, although he did not feel the director's attempt to fuse the
real and the fantastic had been totally successful.[1] There is some irony in even this
positive response, for when critics later changed their minds about the aesthetic
value of the film, it was precisely what Ueno criticized—the mix of genres—that
was most highly praised. Many other critics in Japan, however, found no reason at
first to be impressed with a pictorial flair so long familiar. Neither had they any
particular reason to think much of the screenplay's conflation of two tales from a
nineteenth-century collection of ghost stories, Akinari Ueda's *Ugetsu Monogatari*
(Tales of Moonlight and Rain, 1858). The Japanese had become all too familiar
with attempts to transpose serious literary work to the screen. Since 1937, in fact,
productions of that kind had flooded the market.

    Ugetsu's initially cool reception at home had much to do with the particular
climate of the film industry in Japan during this period. The return of Japanese
sovereignty after the dissolution of the Occupation in 1952 has a direct impact on
the artistic development of the national cinema. Release from the strict censorship
and guidelines instituted by SCAP (Supreme Commander of Allied Powers)
offered filmmakers new flexibility in their choice of subject matter. Many directors turned to contemporary themes, some playing to antiwar sentiments, others to
the conflict between individualism and pressure for social conformity. The resul-

---

1. See Ichiro Ueno, "*Ugetsu Monogatari*" (*Ugetsu*), *Kinema Jumpo*, no. 62 (April 1953): 54–55.

tant blossoming of creativity in this decade marked what has been termed "the Golden Age of postwar Japanese cinema."

For example, Tadashi Imai, a director with communist leanings, was invited by a major studio to make *Himeyuri no To* (*The Tower of Lilies*). This antiwar film about high school girls forced to kill themselves rather than surrender during the invasion of Okinawa was extremely successful. His next film *Nigorie* (*Muddy Waters*) criticized the feudal system of early modern Japan through a portrayal of oppressed women. It was rated best picture of the year by Japan's most prestigious film journal *Kinema Jumpo*. *Yoakemae* (*Before Dawn*) reflected director Kosaburo Yoshimura's evaluation of modern history—the Meiji Restoration seen through the eyes of the common people. Keisuke Kinoshita's *Nihon no Higeki* (*A Japanese Tragedy*) studied how the clash of old and new values opened up a gulf between a poor mother and her children, resulting in the mother's suicide. Kon Ichikawa made *Puusan* (*Mr. Pu*), a satire on the impersonal, competitive modern society that has no place for a good-hearted person. Even Yasujiro Ozu, who persisted in the genre of *shomingeki* (drama about middle-class people), invested *Tokyo Monogatari* (*Tokyo Story*) with a topic consonant with the current trend: the clash of modern and traditional as revealed in the dissolution of a middle-class family. Every one of these films was released in 1953, the same year as *Ugetsu*. Clearly, in the midst of so many films reflecting current issues, Mizoguchi's *Ugetsu* was bound to seem archaic and was consequently easy to dismiss. The general audience, like the critics, was also less than enthusiastic.

Outside Japan, however, where the context for viewing was radically different, the film seemed both novel and brilliant. The very elements (such as the blend of supernatural and realist genres and film techniques) that Japanese audiences took for granted were hailed by foreign critics as evidence that *Ugetsu* was a masterpiece. Thus, the film won Mizoguchi a Silver Lion Award at the Venice Festival in 1953. Gavin Lambert, reporting the event, considered *Ugetsu* a film endowed with the "quality of revelation":

> Like *Rashomon* and *Tora-No-O*, its starting point is a period of civil war and the adventures of a few individuals in an epoch of violence and upheaval, but it combines the purest folklore with its reality. This strange and beautiful work, in which phantoms, friendly and vengeful, magical signs and rituals, coexist with the visible world, has richly delicate images, a powerful dramatic development, and is wonderfully acted by Machi-Ko [sic] Kyo and Masayuki Mori.[2]

Undoubtedly, then, some part of *Ugetsu*'s success in the West derived from Mizoguchi's mode of representation, which seemed uniquely Japanese and

2. Gavin Lambert, "The Festivals—Venice." *Sight and Sound* 23, no. 2 (October–December 1953): 58–59.

uniquely valuable, as Dudley Andrew notes in his introduction to *Kenji Mizoguchi: A Guide to References and Resources:* "In both Japan and the West there exists a view that originality is not a characteristic to be sought in the Japanese artist; rather, the great artists will be those who must thoroughly express some aspects of a national way of doing things or looking at things."[3]

In fact, Mizoguchi's hallmark—the long take—has been widely acclaimed by Western reviewers, who see it as creating the same kind of rhythmic beauty seen in the medieval *emakimono,* or picture scrolls. Interestingly, the French New Wave director Jean-Luc Godard has noticed that Mizoguchi's moving camera creates effects in lighting similar to the touch Hokusai brings to his *ukiyoe* prints. Certain scenes—especially that of the lovers' picnic—stand by themselves as particularly good examples of Mizoguchi's gift for evoking mood. All of these reactions to the "Japaneseness" of the film helped to ensure its success in the West.

Oddly enough, although they were enraptured by technique, critics, like the moviegoing public, did not seriously consider many of the questions that the film posed for them. Although it was not set in the present, was *Ugetsu* supposed to be some kind of parable about the sufferings of individuals in wartime? Did Mizoguchi really intend to give major scenes some kind of convincing supernatural atmosphere? And where was the social realism that made his films of the 1930s so compelling—films like *Naniwa Ereji* (*Osaka Elegy,* 1936) and *Gion no Shimai* (*Sisters of Gion,* 1936)? Even his well-known ambiance—here characterized by lyricism juxtaposed with realistic details of the horrors of war—provoked only a few to serious inquiry. It was enough to recognize and note the existence of that ambiance.

Inspired by *Ugetsu*'s success abroad Japanese critics began to reassess their responses. (In fact, *Ugetsu* was voted the third best picture of the year by *Kinema Jumpo* in early 1954.) Like those critics, when encountering such varied responses to this film, we might ask how one "reads" and "appreciates" such a work. One way to begin is with an overview of Mizoguchi's oeuvre in which this particular film can be placed, especially since *Ugetsu* offers a clear example of Mizoguchi's thematic concerns and aesthetic forms over his many years as a director.

Mizoguchi's Thematic Constants

Mizoguchi's concern for women is recognized as a constant by all knowledgeable viewers of his work. As his surviving films clearly show, that concern is frequently expressed through his depiction of heroines pitted against a male-dominated, money-oriented society. Using that conflict as the driving force of the drama, he

---

3. Dudley and Paul Andrew, *Kenji Mizoguchi: A Guide to References and Resources* (Boston: G. K. Hall, 1961), p. 23.

probes woman's plight, the decisions a woman must make and the relationships that she must endure (or refuse to endure) with men. A typical Mizoguchi heroine either rises up in revolt against a world that exploits her or simply suffers and endures. In either case, she is nearly always victimized by forces beyond her control and seldom emerges triumphant.

For example, *Sisters of the Gion* presents two sisters, one representing a rebellious and one a more passive response to a restrictive society. The elder, Umekichi, accepts the onus of *giri* (social obligation), even when it means being exploited by her former patron. The younger sister, Omocha (her name itself translates as "toy"), despises the Gion, the licensed pleasure district where she works, and all that it stands for. She follows the path of *ninjo* (personal inclination). Rejecting her status as a mere plaything of men, she does all she can to exploit her clients. Each sister follows her principles to equally bitter ends.

A similar theme is worked out in *Gion Bayashi* (Gion Festival Music, 1953, released in the United States as *Geisha*). Here the contrast is between two geisha. The elder, Miyoharu, tries to live according to the norms of geisha society. The younger, Eiko, is a more modern type. She has rebelled against paternal authority and chosen this profession of her own free will, in order to become economically independent. At first, the women's values contrast; but then they merge as the two professional entertainers of men united in refusing the advances of clients bent on exploiting them. Miyoharu and Eiko also share the consequences of their solidarity. Cut off from their sole source of income, each is forced to shift ground and to become reconciled to her fate. What they have lost in hope, however, they gain in a kind of heightened consciousness. They lend one another support, even as they must face the world on its terms (not theirs) and make the best of a bad bargain in life. Their defeat helps create a mother/daughter or elder sister/younger sister bond that promises to become a source of strength. Even so, the conclusion of the film suggests very strongly that the oppressive world in which these two women live remains impersonal and indifferent to their sacrifice.

Mizoguchi portrays many female types, but he is particularly drawn to the fallen woman. He insists, however, on her essential nobility. In some films the form this nobility takes is the woman's sacrificial effort to redeem a morally weak man. This spiritual theme is given its most convincing treatment in two films from the prewar period. In *Taki no Shiraito* (White Threads of the Cascade, released in the United States as *The Water Magician,* 1932), a showgirl, Shiraito, falls in love with a young student. She goes into debt putting him through law school and is later arrested for the murder of the moneylender who demands sexual favors when she cannot repay his loans. The ironic ending of the film shows Shiraito and her student protegé meeting for the last time in court, where she is the defendant, he the prosecutor. *Zangiku Monogatari* (*The Story of the Last Chrysanthemum,* 1939) takes us into the world of Kabuki, with all its remnants of feudal social structure. Here, a young maid, Otoku, who loves an apprentice actor, sacrifices herself to help him become a star. In the typical Shinpa tradition, a melodramatic final scene shows her, still loving and faithful, on her deathbed.[4]

In each of these films, the conclusion shows a man transformed thanks to the noble sacrifice of a woman of lowly status. In *White Threads of the Cascade,* the prosecutor realizes how much the woman's devotion to him has cost her. Instead of taking this as his due, he resigns from the prestigious position that her sacrifice has earned him.[5] In *The Story of the Last Chrysanthemum,* the successful actor visits the dying Otoku, to whom he owes so much. He begs forgiveness for all the misery his selfishness has caused and is shown as a wiser and a better man for his experience. Having taken advantage of a woman's support throughout his career, in the end he learns that fame is not the ultimate reward in life.

All these themes appear in *Ugetsu.* Yet, like *The Life of Oharu,* another of Mizoguchi's best films, *Ugetsu* uses personal issues in order to focus on a more universal level. In this film, the questions of social restriction and injustice are both a matter of individual lives and of masses of humanity struggling to survive oppressive forces in wartime. In a letter to his scriptwriter, Yoshikata Yoda, Mizoguchi wrote about his intentions:

> Whether war originates in the ruler's personal motives, or in some public concern, how violence, disguised as war, oppresses and torments the populace both physically and spiritually! . . . I want to emphasize this as the main theme of the film.[6]

The film's action centers on two possible ways of confronting the Japanese civil wars of the sixteenth century (or, by implication, any major social disruption at any time). The first, represented by Genjuro, Tobei, and to a certain extent, Ohama, Tobei's wife, is the way of opportunistic greed and relinquishment of a sense of rootedness. The second, represented by Miyagi, Genjuro's wife, is the

---

4. In the decade beginning around 1910, Shinpa, whose name translates as New School or New Group, set itself up in opposition to the conventions of Kabuki by offering drama in contemporary settings. Though Shinpa theater incorporated many genres, its forte was tragedy of a sort that later developed into the Japanese equivalent of melodrama. Mizoguchi's earlier films include a number of adaptations of Shinpa tragedies. *Nihonbashi* and *White Threads of the Cascade* are both based on Shinpa plays with those same titles by the Meiji writer Kyoka Izumi.

5. There are three versions of *White Threads of the Cascade* available today. The first version, in the possession of the Film Center of the Tokyo Museum of Modern Art, does not contain Shiraito's dream (in prison) in which she envisions herself smilingly watching carp, a symbol of rising fortune, swimming in a pond, while thinking of her happy reunion with Kinya. It also lacks the final scene of Kinya's suicide, ending instead in his writing a letter of resignation. The second version, which was cut during the Allied Occupation, has a happy ending. The sections of Kinya's sentencing Shiraito and his subsequent suicide are deleted, and the dream scene was added to the end. The final and more complete version, which I saw at the Bungeiza Theater in Tokyo, has both the dream and the suicide scenes.

6. Yoshikata Yoda, *Mizoguchi Kenji no Hito to Geijutsu* (Kenji Mizoguchi: His Life and Art) (Tokyo: Kawabe, 1970), p. 216.

way of endurance that entails devotion to community and optimism about a possibly better future. Given the rigid societal structure of feudal Japan, where geographic mobility was forbidden to the commoner, the first way would normally have been impossible, but the turmoil of civil war itself allowed for such an alternative. The first part of the film focuses on the clash of these opposing values and the resultant dissolution of the family, while the second half shows Genjuro's obsession with illusion and the eventual restoration of the family. These themes are explored through the depiction of each character's attitudes toward money, when wartime provides rare opportunities for riches.

The power of money to pit wife against husband and woman against woman is first glimpsed when Genjuro and Tobei return from their first pottery-selling trip. Genjuro boasts about the value of this windfall for his family. His wife, Miyagi, warns him not to be greedy. She values family solidarity more than material gain. Genjuro's goal of grasping opportunity when it is offered transforms him for the worse, as others (who uphold family and community ties) observe. The wise village headman is quick to point out that money earned in time of civil unrest soon flies away.

Genjuro's change of character is underlined by the clash between Miyagi and Ohama, who represent two women's points of view. As Miyagi laments her husband's transformation, Ohama joins the two men in defending their spirit of opportunism. This scene also maps out the course each woman is to take as events unfold. Ohama supports the materialistic drive by joining the men on their selling expedition. Miyagi plays the part of the submissive wife, following her husband's orders to remain behind. Thus hers is the path of traditional endurance—which in her case leads to death. Tobei's ambition leads him to a mistaken attempt to raise not only his income but his social status. Significantly, Ohama, who is otherwise supportive, opposes this. They clash when Tobei decides to buy the suit of armor he needs to become the great samurai of his dreams.

Mizoguchi can be counted on to pursue these themes, and others I have mentioned, to their bitter ends. Each woman becomes a victim of male selfishness, first by being made vulnerable to the hazards of war through separation from her husband. After Ohama becomes the victim of roaming samurai, we next see her working in a brothel. This section of the film works through two familiar narrative patterns in Mizoguchi's work. Throughout the film Ohama has been presented as aggressive in counterpoint to the submissive Miyagi. Now, with Tobei looking on, we see her relentlessly pursue a nonpaying client in order to get the money that is due her. Her actions here show that Ohama has mettle enough to turn each stage of her suffering into some act of aggression in defiance of her male oppressors.

This same sequence is a moment of truth or redemption for Tobei as well. He is suddenly, and rather easily, reduced from a would-be samurai to his true status as peasant. Any resistance he might have felt gives way to Ohama's accusations. Yet even as she berates him for his selfishness, we see that her fallen status has not, in fact, compromised her wifely devotion at all. (Most of Mizoguchi's fallen women share this degree of fidelity.) Ohama says: "I wanted to kill myself so many times, but I couldn't because I wanted to see you just one more time. I hated myself for that desire." The two are shown by the director to be reconciled, although they can never change the past.

In the case of Genjuro, commonplace greed has been replaced by sensual abandon in the arms of the demonic Lady Wakasa. Miyagi, abandoned to fend for herself and her child, is attacked by army deserters who want the little bit of food she possesses. In the struggle, she is killed. Family values are brought very much to the fore in this plot line. Eventually, Miyagi and Genjuro are reconciled in a scene confirming her familial role as a devoted wife and mother. Here, Miyagi's nobly forgiving character allows her even as a ghost to keep watch over her family. All the signs of Miyagi's compassion—cooking a meal for the husband who has abandoned her and mending his kimono—are clearly present when Genjuro returns to their hut. She says simply: "Don't say another word. You are back safe now. That's all that matters."

Once again, the wife's forgiveness conjoins with the husband's growing self-knowledge to effect his redemption. Genjuro first glimpses the truth when he discovers the identity of Princess Wakasa and recognizes that he has been immersed in a phantasmal world. This knowledge signals the end of his pursuit of passion and motivates a return to the family and its values. With the village headman's announcement of Miyagi's death (after Genjuro has seen her presence in their house), there is a corresponding transition from supernatural back to natural. Earlier, we saw Genjuro walking among the ruins of Wakasa's mansion. Here, we see him sitting alone with his son in his war-damaged hut. It is through a highly stylized technique and combination of seemingly conflicting modes of representation, corresponding to the supernatural and realistic, that these many themes are presented.

Stylistics/Modes of Representation

The theme of the individual's confrontation with a chaotic feudal society in sixteenth-century Japan might be expected to yield a glossy historical film or perhaps a highly realistic, politically committed, near-documentary, yet Mizoguchi's approach is quite different. He engages with his material on several levels—realistic, aesthetic, religious, and mystical—in a uniquely successful integration of themes and styles. To begin with, there are two "realities" made use of in *Ugetsu:* the natural world, most tangibly present in a world at war; and the supernatural world of ghosts and apparitions. This duality calls forth a range of expressive devices in similar contrast, moving back and forth between unvarnished realism and highly stylized lyricism. Some of the resulting scenes could stand by themselves as proofs of Mizoguchi's mastery in this difficult art of shifting and intersecting perspectives. He is always at his richest and best using familiar techniques—the long take, for which his work is famous; the long shot; the pan; the dissolve; and low-key photography generally. To these might be added a special felicity of camera movement, the fluid glide from one segment to the next, resulting in a pleasing control of the total effects of pictorial composition.

In the first half of the film, Mizoguchi portrays the collective misery that the war has brought on the villagers. In order to do this, he creates an appropriate mood through a combination of low-key photography and many long and medium shots. For example, only the fronts of the houses in the village are illuminated; everything else about them and the street remains obscure. Against this backdrop, he presents a series of long shots of the villagers heading for cover. By not using a close-up of a single person, he emphasizes collective, not individual fear. In spite of this focus on the collective, this dark texture draws us into the village environment, making us feel the villagers' suffering as something immediate to our own experience. Mizoguchi, in fact, considered darker textures generally more effective in sustaining audience concentration on a film's action because such textures create a sense of close-framing or enclosure rather than open framing, which allows attention to wander.

In those scenes of the film that are more focused on the two women, each one's moral conflict is conveyed by a variety of expressive devices. For example, throughout the early shots of *Ugetsu* Mizoguchi uses the close-up very rarely, but he uses it very effectively later on in the sequence featuring the villagers' escape. While other villagers flee toward the mountain, Miyagi rushes into the house to get her boy out of bed and grasp him in her arms. A sudden close-up of her face fixes Miyagi in our minds as the quintessential sufferer of wartime—as both an individual and a representative example: the mother whose love for her family serves as a standard that we use to measure the worst that can be done to outrage human feelings in time of war.

The scene of Genjuro's separation from his wife and child not only reinforces the division between opportunism and resignation, but provides another example of Mizoguchi's vision of the wife left behind. Here, he uses the rigorously objective camera, subtly modified by his lyrical bent. Initially, cross-cutting between the husband in the boat and Miyagi on the shore—a standard method for rendering relationships—elucidates the mutual caring of husband and wife, soon to be endangered. After further intercutting between Miyagi and the other passengers, Mizoguchi lets the camera track along with Miyagi as she walks along the shore to see the party off. When she stops, the camera stops too, and its extended look, in a long shot, falls on Miyagi still standing among the tall grass watching the boat, now off screen. The *nouvelle vague* director Nagisa Oshima once said Mizoguchi could express his thoughts and feelings only through the camera. This observation seems especially appropriate for this scene. Mizoguchi has moved his camera as if he were compassionately watching this poor woman's plight, and we feel sympathy for her. A fade—the typical Mizoguchi punctuation—follows the long shot of Miyagi, underscoring the elegiac mood appropriate to her sorrow.

Mizoguchi later presents Ohama's moral quandary in a similar fashion, a convincing example being the rape sequence. The roaming samurais' assault on her takes place in a devastated temple. As before, the director lets the camera do the talking. As Ohama bursts into tears, surrounded by samurai, the camera swiftly cuts back to the outside of the temple as if it could not bear to see her raped. Instead, it presents a close-up of Ohama's discarded straw sandals to allow us to imagine what is happening inside.

Mizoguchi is known for his sensitivity to every detail of a woman's movements and uses those movements, in a manner analogous to the monosyllabic eloquence of Ozu's male characters, to say more than words can about her feelings and the experiences she endures. Thus, in the scene that immediately follows Ohama's rape, the film's action dignifies her suffering partly through the director's controlled study of her figure, especially her back. When she leaves the temple after the samurais' departure, the No chorus vocalizes her sorrow and indignation. Just as in Miyagi's case, the camera follows straightforwardly, taking its cues from her motions. The next image is an apt example of what a single image can do to elicit a rich response. A low-angle shot shows Ohama standing in the door of the temple; she is looking up at the sky with her back to us. Her disheveled figure fits in with the desolate surroundings: the ruined temple and the gloomy sky with a waning moon. The shot creates the effect of a Chinese ink paining, while the fusion of Ohama and her environment externalize her emotional state as articulated by the No chorus. The mood that is created helps draw us into her mind more effectively than a close-up of her face could do. Furthermore, the entire filmic composition, especially the low-angle shot, makes it appear as though Mizoguchi were looking up to Ohama, admiring her courage to struggle through life.

Another technique in which Mizoguchi is expert, and to which I have previously referred, is the art of shifting and intersecting the "realistic" and the "mystical." The boat scene, the most famous segment of the film, is often cited as a high point of such mastery. To open the scene, Mizoguchi employs a long shot of the boat emerging from the mist. The difficulty of distinguishing any object clearly, in itself, engenders a supernatural mood, which is further enhanced by Ohama's monotonous singing that merges with distant drumbeats. The drum, in turn, is interrupted from time to time by the sound of distant guns. This sound reminds us of the reality of war as experienced by the two families in the boat. Turning 90 degrees, the boat reveals its side to us. Mizoguchi's famous one-scene, one-shot method follows, fixing our attention on the five in the boat; they and it are completely subsumed into a general texture of gray, as mist slowly erases contrast.

As the supernatural atmosphere gradually wanes, the film takes on a highly realistic dimension, both visually and auditorily. The men in the boat, drinking sake, begin to speak of capitalizing on the war by selling the pottery they have salvaged from the burning of their village. In contrast, Miyagi nibbles her food in silence, her face expressing sad resignation. Suddenly, the long take yields to a shifting perspective as the realistic texture recedes. The supernatural atmosphere returns again as a point-of-view shot reveals a strange boat approaching from the distance. The mist still hovers over the lake. Though Mizoguchi uses wide-framing here, this dark texture creates the effect of close-framing. It steeps everything in a kind of supernatural ambience, in which we sympathetically experience the passengers' felt reality: a sense of approaching danger. The drum-beats become louder and louder, as Ohama's singing diminishes. A long shot of the two boats almost stern to stern quietly gives way to a medium shot of both.

The passengers in the boat think that the mysterious vessel is haunted by ghosts. Our expectation of the supernatural, like theirs, however, is broken when a man in the boat explains that he has been attacked by pirates, adding that they will take everything, especially women. The transition to realism is abrupt. A swift cut to the two women's anxious faces is followed by a medium shot of all concerned gathering around the dying boatman. Here too, the drumbeats do their work: we seem to hear the very heartbeats of these terrified people in the grip of the war's immediacy.

The latter half of *Ugetsu* shows a similar juxtaposition of styles. The thematic change in Genjuro's story starts with a long shot of Lady Wakasa and her attendant leading him into her mansion. The supernatural aura is already present in the princess's face, which resembles the female No mask; and her gait is of an unearthly lightness like that of a ghost in No drama. Mizoguchi employs an unusually long track to show the three going down the street, through a field and into the garden of Wakasa's mansion. Here as elsewhere, Mizoguchi's incorpora-tion of the female No mask is quite effective and economical in creating a supernatural aura. Although some scholars claim that the female No mask is virtually expressionless because it represents what may be called "neutral expres-sion" or "intermediate expression," it is brought to life by angles of reflection from the stage (or, here, the cinematographer's light)—expressive refractions the highly skilled performer can use to convey a multitude of emotions. (It might be noted here that the female No mask is not really symmetrical. Seen close-up, one half reveals a bright, lively expression, while the other is sad and melancholy. Taken together, these offer the expression that is "neutral"—until the mask is deployed just so. A lowering of the mask, for example, is *kumorasu,* and casts shadows suggestive of grief; similarly, *terasu* is raising of the mask to lighten and create suggestions of happiness. *Kiru* refers to a sudden movement of the mask to right or left, expressive of anger.) All these formalistic aspects of No drama join together to reveal Lady Wakasa's character. While her mask of a face—bewitch-ingly elegant and beautiful—remains cold and impassive, it evokes a variety of suppressed passions. Needless to say, the film's texture, camera movement, and Wakasa's own movements all help Mizoguchi achieve the effects he desires.

At the mansion, the film pictorially reinforces our sense of the supernatural. As Genjuro is guided down the long corridor (reminiscent of the No passageway) to a back room, there is a slow cross-cutting between his room and the others along the way. Darkness prevails, then yields to a soft illumination as Wakasa's servants light candles in the open rooms. The timing of this textual contrast is so calculated that we are struck by the beauty of the composition. In two scenes depicting Wakasa's relationship with Genjuro, the supernatural mood is sustained. The combined use of acoustics, the No convention, and the high-angle camera unite to become superbly effective, enhancing the individual characters' deliberately calculated movements. The first scene involves Wakasa's seduction of Genjuro. Her face is again made up like an immobile female No mask. The elderly attendant, attired in a black kimono, sits closest, with her back to the camera. Her stature is as imposing as that of the princess herself, clad in a white kimono, seated as if to block Genjuro, who is farthest from the camera. Sinister chimes—perhaps of a bell for Buddhist prayers—are heard intermittently. As Wakasa takes a drink of sake from a small wine cup, we hear the chime. When Genjuro follows suit, we hear it again, as if to indicate that the bell marks each stage of his moral decline. During the subsequent giving in—a lovely play chase—Mizoguchi makes sure that Wakasa stands high above Genjuro, whose lower position enhances a sense of his entrapment in her snares. The final shot shows him collapsing to the floor with her.

The soundtrack, as elsewhere in the film, reinforces the supernatural aura of this vignette. Wakasa's wedding song gradually merges with what sounds like a priest's low-toned prayer from a No play, accompanied by a wooden drum used for prayers. The camera quickly dollies from the center of the room to the corner to show us a suit of black armor, the source of the mysterious incantation. The voice is the spirit of Wakasa's father, still haunting the mansion. The merging of songs by Wakasa and the spirit conjure up an image of death for the lovers' doomed affair.

This first scene of the lovers' union is more profitably viewed in relation to the later scene depicting Wakasa's anger at Genjuro's desertion after his discovery that she is a ghost. Again, the camera's high angle and Wakasa's domineering posture heighten our sense of the snare from which Genjuro is desperate to escape. Discordant music combines with the Lady Wakasa's black attire to further enhance the sinister atmosphere. The culmination of his struggle is shown in close-up from a high angle with the lady and her attendant looking reproachfully down at a sutra painted on Genjuro's back. Here, the static masklike face undergoes a sudden transformation. Mizoguchi uses a shot-by-shot alternation in order to reveal Wakasa's true identity.[7]

Two other important sequences reveal Mizoguchi's cinematic signs of Genjuro's moral conflict. One is the sequence of the lovers bathing and their subsequent repose on the lawn. This sequence represents the culmination of Genjuro's passion. Genjuro is soaking himself in the spring while Wakasa is still ashore. Holding her hands, he tells her that he has never had such a wonderful experience. The camera follows Wakasa as she momentarily steps into the woods to take off

7. Audie Bock, *Japanese Film Directors* (Tokyo: Kodansha International, 1976), p. 49.

her clothes and returns to him. At the moment when they are about to embrace in the spring, Mizoguchi's camera moves uneasily.[8] It quickly moves away from them and ends with a dissolve, as if to say that the director himself is averting his eyes from this spectacle of moral disarray. This traveling pan is in strong contrast with the earlier slower dolly and pan shots, which imply Mizoguchi's sympathy for both Ohama and Miyagi. It is counterpoised with a diagonal tracking shot which Mizoguchi uses to register Genjuro's repentance when he finds himself in the ruins of the mansion and thinks of starting homeward to Miyagi.[9]

After the dissolve that ends the scene at the spring, the camera dollies toward the bushes of a garden with raked white sand, and then moves up to show a long shot of Genjuro and Wakasa on the lawn. The garden looks like the stone garden of Ryoanji or that of Daisenin Temple, both noted Zen temples in Kyoto. An extremely brief shot of the garden is charged with a philosophical undertone: the garden stands by itself, transcending all petty human affairs. As happens occasionally in the film, Mizoguchi reaches beyond the juxtaposition between the real and the unreal as if, in this case, to emphasize a removal from both the supernatural and the mundane to something higher and more universal.

In the following sequence, Wakasa and Genjuro are seen having a picnic on a blanket spread on the lawn, flooded with warm spring sunlight. The shot itself is pictorially beautiful, and the very essence of Mizoguchi's lyricism. The abrupt transition from the shadow in the bath scene to the light, with short stasis in between, and from closed framing to open framing as well, creates a kind of leisurely visual pleasure for the viewer. The same effect is produced again when Genjuro begins chasing Wakasa; the couple, clad in very light silk kimonos, look like two fluttering butterflies merging with the spring air.

Another lyrical sequence is Genjuro's reunion with his wife, now a ghost. Mizoguchi once more relies on an admixture of the supernatural and the actual to present the qualities of a woman: in this case, the nobly forgiving source of the most rewarding form of man's redemption. As in many other scenes, the transition from natural to supernatural is made so surreptitiously that the audience is taken by surprise. When Genjuro comes home, he enters the dark, deserted house. He goes out through the back door, and when the camera pans back to the interior again, we are surprised to see Miyagi (whom we earlier saw killed) sitting near the brightly burning hearth. After the husband and child are asleep, the slowly moving camera and extreme low-key photography yield a mixture of tenderness and eeriness. Only a tiny spot of light from Miyagi's candle moves from place to place as she moves around the house, while the rest of the screen is dominated by

8. Joan Mellen, *The Waves at Genji's Door: Japan Through Its Cinema* (New York: Pantheon, 1976), pp. 103–104.
9. Ibid., p 103.

darkness. We see her starting to patch her husband's kimono—the gesture indicative of female caring, her smiling face meeting the darkness.

Cultural Approaches to the Final Scene: Integration of Form and Content

The final scene, which consists of four shots, resolves the issues of opportunism and resignation, and seems to strive for an almost religious response from the viewer. Genjuro is shown working at the potter's wheel and feeding the kiln with wood. The scene ends with a long take of events outside Genjuro's house. The liquid camera movement again has the effect of a picture scroll unfolding. Mizoguchi makes use of the freedom of open framing made possible by the mobile camera. The exterior of the potter's house is presented first. Formerly barren, it now appears transformed into a farm, which Tobei is cultivating. This shot echoes the earlier scene when he realized the futility of climbing the social ladder. Ohama is busily cooking a meal while Genjuro is feeding the kiln. The camera follows the little boy going toward his mother's grave and stops as he kneels before it. It then pans up and travels across the field to show the entire community.

The final scene is rich in meaning deftly condensed, inviting reflection on war's effects on four individuals and their village. Here we come to accept that in a time of civil war, two conflicting ways of adapting to the environment were equally impossible to realize. The film's world view is basically ironic: given such chaos, the individual cannot prevail, no matter what kind of action he or she takes. Survival is dependent on chance alone. Miyagi's option, with which Mizoguchi sympathizes, is less rewarding than those taken by the others. Although Tobei, Genjuro, and Ohama have been defeated in their aims, they have survived; their very defeat has taught them the insignificance of all "options." Yet, Miyagi rises, through death, above the merely tragic: she becomes the most sublime type of woman, the one who *can* forgive. The shot of Genjuro busily engaged in loading the kiln is accompanied by Miyagi in a voice-over: "So much has happened to us. Now at last you have become the man I hoped you would be." There is redemption for Genjuro, as well, in this thought.

A crane shot of the entire village implies a deeper and more universal philosophical idea, the concept of *mujo* (the mutability of all earthy phenomena), strongly rooted in Buddhism. Two important elements make this vision possible. Earlier in the film, the view has been anticipated in Princess Wakasa's singing. At the wedding her song is: "The finest silk of rarest shade / May fade away, and quickly, too / So may the love I offer you, / If your heart proves false to me." The same song is recalled by Genjuro, as he roams around the ramparts of the mansion. Her song certainly points to the transitoriness of all human affairs, a theme that underlies most of traditional Japanese literature. *Mujo* is also a staple Buddhist idea expressed in No drama, the conventions of which Mizoguchi has made use in earlier scenes.

The conclusion of *Ugetsu* reinforces the classical idea of *mujo* through another traditional trope: the rotating wheel (representing the concept of a perpetual cycle, as opposed to a teleological belief in history, with a beginning, middle, and end). In the earlier sequence permeated by the cozy domestic atmosphere, both Genjuro and Miyagi turn the potter's wheel, this movement synchronized to music on the sound track. Here at the end, amid the peaceful atmosphere after civil war, Genjuro spins the wheel alone, while his deceased wife's voice is heard encouraging him to make good pottery. The physical absence of Miyagi acutely echoes the idea of impermanence. Then too, time, symbolized by the wheel, transcends all human affairs. The film begins and ends with a shot of the mountain village. The tension of war and the serenity of a tentative peace in the future are thus presented as part of the cyclical pattern working itself out in the fullness of time.

Kenji Mizoguchi: A Biographical Sketch

enji Mizoguchi was born on May 16, 1898, in Yushima Nihana-cho, Hongo, Tokyo—a middle-class district. His father was a carpenter and roofer. He had a sister seven years older and a brother seven years younger. When Mizoguchi was seven, his father went bankrupt, sold their home, and moved the family to Asakusa, the plebeian downtown Tokyo area. Poverty also forced the father to put his fourteen-year-old daughter up for adoption at a geisha house and, shortly thereafter, to send the eleven-year-old Kenji to northern Japan to live with relatives. As a result, Mizoguchi attended school for just six years—a handicap that burdened him with feelings of inferiority long after he had achieved success in films.

By the time of Mizoguchi's mother's death in 1915, he had become alienated from his father, while growing increasingly dependent on his sister. After becoming a geisha, Suzu was "redeemed" by Count Matsudaira, first to be his mistress and then his wife. Through Suzu's influence, Mizoguchi was apprenticed to a designer of patterns for summer kimonos. He must have displayed some interest and talent in design, for Suzu subsequently sent her brother to study Western painting in the studio of Kiyoteru Kuroda, who worked in the new impressionist manner. Undoubtedly, Mizoguchi's early training in the visual arts had much to do with his notable sense of composition as a filmmaker.

But literature, along with dramatic adaptations of literary works, left their mark as well, for Mizoguchi was a wide-ranging and attentive reader from his early years. He particularly admired such nineteenth-century European writers as Leo

There are a number of biographies of Mizoguchi written in Japanese. Yoshikata Yoda's seminal work, *Mizoguchi Kenji no Hito to Geijutsu* (Kenji Mizoguchi: His Life and Art) (Tokyo: Kawabe, 1970) traces this giant filmmaker's contradictory life as it interacts with his art. The director Kaneto Shindo's book *Aru Eiga Kantoku: Mizoguchi Kenji to Nihon Eiga* (A Film Director: Kenji Mizoguchi and Japanese Film) (Tokyo: Iwanami, 1976), along with his film *Aru Eiga Kantoku no Shogai* (Kenji Mizoguchi: The Life of a Film Director, 1975), are striking revelations of the crucial incidents in Mizoguchi's career, which most affected him as a director and as a man.

Tolstoy, Emile Zola, and Guy de Maupassant, along with the major Mejii novelists Soseki Natsume, Koyo Ozaki, Kyoka Izumi, and Kafu Nagai. Maupassant and Kafu led him to value the methods of naturalism, a perspective that was fostered by his own childhood memories of poverty and dislocation as well as by a brief period of newspaper work in Kobe, where he became more sharply aware of the realities of urban slum life. At the same time, his reading of the novels of Tolstoy and Soseki stimulated a philosophical awareness of life, while Koyo's works and the narrative *kodan* (stories of heroic exploits) drew him toward the allegorical treatment of human experience, something that Mizoguchi paradoxically combined with his inclinations toward naturalism.

Mizoguchi's personal and literary experience during this period also helped to develop his lifelong fascination with the sufferings of women. His own dependency on Suzu, who by now had taken on the burden of supporting her entire family, probably led him to his interest in the melodramatic Mejii novelist Kyoka, whose work often revolved around female devotion and the pangs of unrequited love. Mizoguchi also displayed a great interest in Shinpa, a popular form of drama that differed from Kabuki in its use of contemporary settings and situations. The focus of Shinpa concerned tragedies that make "a grand display of the ego or will of a woman who endures her fate in tears."[1]

While Mizoguchi's sense of the world was evolving at this time, what he would do in the world was still in question. He seemed to be drifting, never staying with any occupation for long, and making no effort to seek a career. As a result, a turning point in Mizoguchi's life came about virtually by chance. Through an acquaintance who was a *biwa* teacher and occasional actor, he met Osamu Wakayama, a director at the Nikkatsu Studio, the dominant studio of the time. Wakayama was persuaded to hire the twenty-one-year-old Mizoguchi as his assistant.

Mizoguchi's arrival at Nikkatsu was opportune because this conservative studio, responding to its competitors, was at last becoming receptive to innovation; most significantly, Nikkatsu began to use actresses in place of the female impersonators who had customarily played women's roles. The female impersonators went on strike and the studio then decided to exclude them permanently.

Mizoguchi benefited from this momentary turmoil as well as from the more general changes in the way films were made and in the narratives they presented. Just two months after he became an assistant director, at the age of twenty-four, he made his first film: *Ai ni Yomigaeru Hi* (*The Resurrection of Love,* 1923). In it, Mizoguchi dispensed with the traditional *benshi* narrator-commentator who accompanied silent film performances; instead he used subtitles and cinematography designed to do the work of narrative film more directly—a radical notion for the time.

---

1. Tadao Sato, *Mizoguchi Kenji no Sekai* (The World of Kenji Mizoguchi) (Tokyo: Tsukuma Shobo, 1982), p. 82.

Films were made quickly in those early days (the average shooting time for a film in a Japanese studio was one week), and Mizoguchi's year of apprenticeship was the most prolific of his life. He made eleven films in genres ranging from mystery stories to psychological drama. Several were based on Western sources, including an adaptation of Eugene O'Neill's *Anna Christie*.

The Great Kanto Earthquake of September 1923 demolished the Nikkatsu Studio and led the company to regroup through a merger with its Taishogun Studio in Kyoto. As a Tokyoite, Mizoguchi at first felt out of place in the genteel climate of the ancient capital, but he came to love its traditional atmosphere and settled there for the rest of his life.

Mizoguchi continued to direct for Nikkatsu-Taishogun throughout the silent period, making many films, most of them routine studio assignments. The exact number is difficult to establish: many studio records were destroyed in World War II bombings, some films of the period did not receive newspaper notice, and Mizoguchi's own memories of his early work were often hazy. It is also difficult to establish a critical estimate of his work in the silent period, since neither prints nor scripts of these films, with one exception, survive. However, we do know that among the many films he made during that time, there were several that received recognition from *Kinema Jumpo*, Japan's leading film journal. *Kaminingyo Haru no Sasayaki* (*A Paper Doll's Whisper of Spring*, 1926), a story of thwarted marriage plans, was praised for its naturalistic treatment of the conflicts created by male egotism and frustrated love, and Mizoguchi regarded it as an important step in his development. *Tokai Kokyogaku* (*Metropolitan Symphony*, 1929) was a *keiko eiga* or "tendency film," that is, one based on the newly emerging proletarian literature of Japan. The script was drawn from works by several proletarian writers and concerned a poor boy and girl who are victimized by the rich and who try to avenge themselves on the wealthy. The film was admired, despite being heavily censored before its release. Its overt political interest is uncharacteristic of Mizoguchi; it is his only authentic "tendency" film.

By 1930 Mizoguchi was making sound films. His first, *Furusato* (*Home Town*), the story of a singer who is first tempted by and then rejects a life in high society, was hampered by the relatively primitive state of early sound technology. But during the thirties, Mizoguchi became more confident of his own talent and more ambitious in the projects he undertook. The change is evident in several ways. He now made fewer films, usually two or even one a year. He became a perfectionist, making extreme demands on cast and crew, and he was painstaking in his supervision of every aspect of production. These tendencies, which some were to label "diabolic," were already noted by Shigeto Miki, his cameraman for *Taki no Shiraito* (*The Water Magician*, 1933), who recalled: "He was a demon when he worked on the film. . . . He caused a lot of trouble for those who worked for him. . . . He would never compromise."[2]

---

2. Quoted by Shindo in *Aru Eiga Kantoku*, p. 121.

Mizoguchi's refusal to compromise led him to move from one Kyoto company to another during the thirties. When Nikkatsu began to dictate terms to directors, he left them in 1932 for Shinko Kinema, and after a brief return to Nikkatsu in 1934, he moved again, this time to Daiichi Eiga; by 1937, he had returned to Shinko. These shifts were partly connected with the financial instability of the film industry during the thirties and partly with Mizoguchi's desire for independent control of his films; as he became an unremitting perfectionist on the set, he more stubbornly resisted external controls by the studio.

The result of Mizoguchi's greater freedom was a greater consistency in the quality of his films. He depended either on his own script ideas, on the works of Kyoka and Soseki, Mejii writers he had always favored, or on the popular novels of Matsutaro Kawaguchi, a close friend. In the mid-thirties he discovered a scenarist, Yoshikata Yoda, who would be his trusted collaborator for two decades. Yoda has written about his working relationship with Mizoguchi (a sample of Mizoguchi's directives to Yoda is included in this volume) and Yoda's recollections portray Mizoguchi's distinctive combination of directorial qualities: he was an insistently demanding martinet who nevertheless rarely gave specific instructions, only the verdict that a scene or a passage was simply not good enough.

Yoda's first collaborations with Mizoguchi took place in 1936 and the two films released in that year—*Naniwa Ereji* (*Osaka Elegy*) and *Gion no Shimai* (*Sisters of the Gion*)—both focused on realistic portrayals of the sufferings of lower-class women. Both films were widely admired; they were awarded third and first place respectively in the annual *Kinema Jumpo* competition, marking the most significant public acknowledgment up to that time of Mizoguchi's gifts as a director. Mizoguchi himself referred to these films as a breakthrough, enabling him for the first time to reveal his sense of how life was actually perceived and experienced. *Osaka Elegy* was Mizoguchi's fifty-sixth film, and it gave him an opportunity to free himself from the Meiji literary tradition with which he had long been concerned. For the first time, his eyes were opened to the possibilities of his new environment, the Kansai area, whose people were different in character and temperament from the Tokyoites he knew so well from his youth.

Just at the point when Mizoguchi established his leadership in Japanese film, the military government made the political climate highly unfavorable to Mizoguchi's pessimistic attitude toward social transformation and improvement. After being forced to direct a patriotic potboiler, *Roei no Uta* (*The Song of the Camp*, 1937), Mizoguchi resigned and moved on to the Schochiku Ofuna Studio, where a freer atmosphere gave him the opportunity to undertake an ambitious trilogy set in the world of classical theater and far removed from current political pressures. These films: *Zangiku Monogatari* (*The Story of the Last Chrysanthemum*); *Naniwa Onna* (*The Woman of Osaka*); *Geido Ichidai Otoko* (*The Life of an Actor*), made between 1939 and 1941, used the world of the Kabuki theater and the Bunraku puppet theater to dramatize the complex interrelationships between art and life.

In *The Woman of Osaka* Mizoguchi cast Kinuyo Tanaka as his heroine. This choice led to one of the happiest personal and professional relationships of his life. His most lasting earlier relationships with women had been turbulent: during the twenties, he had lived with a waitress who stabbed him in the aftermath of a domestic argument and whom he later abandoned to a life of prostitution; his marriage in the thirties ended when his wife had to be committed to a mental hospital. But Tanaka was important to Mizoguchi both professionally and personally; she was the leading actress in many of his later films, including *Ugetsu,* and he was platonically in love with her until the day he died. He drove her as mercilessly as any of his other performers, but he also regarded her with an open and even naive admiration. Their relationship terminated in 1954 when Mizoguchi was openly critical of Tanaka's effort to pursue a career as a film director.

By 1941, Mizoguchi was forced to cooperate with the wartime government, principally by undertaking the direction of several samurai action films. Even though the first of these projects, a monumental two-part saga *Genroku Chushingura (The Loyal 47 Ronin,* 1941–1942), was a qualified artistic success, the director seemed to find the subject and the elaborate demands for an epic staging uncongenial, and the picture never attracted a substantial audience. Two other wartime assignments, both samurai action films, were even less convincing and were subsequently disowned by Mizoguchi.

At the end of the war, Mizoguchi was briefly involved in studio politics; he was elected president of the first labor union organized at the Shochiko Ofuna Studio. But his personal reticence combined uneasily with a desire for the kind of dictatorial authority he pursued as a director; he quickly realized his unsuitability for the presidency and resigned. The films he made during the immediate postwar period were also under governmental restrictions, in this case imposed by the U.S. occupation forces. Several of the films from this 1946–1949 period were strongly feminist (for example, the aptly named *Josei no Shori* [*The Victory of Women,* 1946]), and conformed to the Allied demand that Japanese films support the values of a democratic society. But however compelling the image of the struggling or rebellious woman had always been for Mizoguchi, the celebration of women's achievement of personal freedom did not accord with the director's darker view of human limitations. His most effective film during the occupation was *Utamaro o Meguru Gonin no Onna (Utamaro and His Five Women,* 1946), a period drama about a nineteenth-century artist whom Mizoguchi portrays as a representative of the people.

In the 1950s Mizoguchi achieved a new kind of professional stability and broke out of a period of creative frustration. His work through most of the fifties was produced by a single company (Daiei) after a long period of shifting affiliations; he continued his association with the devoted Yoda as his scenarist and, after 1951, he developed a similar bond with Kazuo Miyagawa as his cinematographer. Through the early fifties, Kinuyo Tanaka remained his leading actress. Perhaps as a result of this continuing collaborative effort, Mizoguchi was able to achieve a consistency in his work that was lacking in his earlier career. As a consequence, his genius began to be recognized

internationally. *Saikaku Ichidai Onna* (*The Life of Oharu*, 1952) won the Venice Film Festival International Prize, and in the following two years Mizoguchi received major awards at Venice for *Ugetsu Monogatari* (*Ugetsu*, 1953) and *Sansho Dayu* (*Sansho the Bailiff*, 1954). Such recognition, for films that were initially less acclaimed in his own country, established Mizoguchi as the most honored of Japanese directors, the first to become widely known outside Japan.

Mizoguchi's renown brought him a seat on the board of directors of the Daiei Company, and he also received a Purple Ribbon Medal from the government for his contributions to the Japanese film industry. But he was now experiencing failing health. By 1955 he knew he was seriously ill, but not yet that he had leukemia. He made several elaborate period films during 1954–1955, despite the onset of his illness, including the masterful *Chikamatsu Monogatari* (*The Crucified Lovers*). *Akasen Chitai* (*Street of Shame*, 1956) was Mizoguchi's last completed film; his condition was worsening, and he needed daily injections on the set to keep him from hemorrhaging. Remarkably, Mizoguchi drove himself to undertake a new project in May of 1956. This was to be *Osaka Monogatari* (*The Tale of Osaka*), a film about a miser's tyrannical hold over his family. When Mizoguchi had to be hospitalized without knowing that his case was terminal, shooting was ostensibly postponed for two months. The great filmmaker died on August 24, 1956, at the age of fifty-eight. In the words of another great filmmaker, Akira Kurosawa, "in the death of Mizoguchi, Japanese film lost its truest creator."[3]

---

3. Quoted in Donald Richie, *The Films of Akira Kurosawa* (Berkeley and Los Angeles: University of California Press, 1973), p. 97. Also quoted by Audie Bock in *Japanese Film Directors* (Tokyo: Kodansha International, 1978), p. 35.

Ugetsu

Ugetsu

The original script was written by Yoshikata Yoda and Matsutaro Kawaguchi. Mizoguchi, however, followed his famous tendency to improvise, making a number of changes in dialogue and action during shooting.

The most signficant departure from the script is in the final sequence of the film. The script focused on Genjuro feeding the kiln, Genichi by his side, with assistance from Ohama. Miyagi's voice provided spiritual guidance as the script concluded with a long shot of the quiet village, chimney smoke rising from it. Mizoguchi modified the characters' actions and, deftly supported by fluid camera movement, altered the *mise-en-scène*.

The continuity script is taken from the U.S. release print, identical to the domestic release except for the addition of subtitles.

For better translations in this volume I have consulted Joanne Bernardi's accurate rendition of the original script.

Camera distance, placement, and movement will be indicated by the following abbreviations:

E L S	extreme long shot (landscape or other large spatial entity; human figures are subordinate to the total field)
L S	long shot (ranging from the totality of a unified, room-sized decor to the whole human figure)
M S	medium shot (human figure from the knees or waist up)
M C U	medium close-up (head and shoulders/chest)
C U	close-up (the whole of a face, other part of body, or object)
E C U	extreme close-up (section of the face, other part of the body or object)
P O V	point of view
(off)	the face of the speaker is off-screen

Credits

Director
Kenji Mizoguchi

Producer
Masaichi Nagata

Planning
Hisakazu Tsuji

Production Company
Daiei

Screenplay
Matsutaro Kawaguchi and
 Yoshikata Yoda

Director of Photography
Kazuo Miyagawa

Assistant Director of Photography
Shozo Tanaka

Art Director
Kisaku Ito

Assistant Art Director
Yasuo Iwaki

Assistant Director
Tokuzo Tanaka

Scenery
Tasaburo Ota

Setting
Uichiro Yamamoto

Wardrobe
Shima Yoshimi

Music
Fumio Hayasaka

Music Assistant
Ichiro Saito

Sound
Iwao Otani

Sound Assistant
Teru Suzuki

Lighting
Kenichi Okamoto

Lighting Assistant
Seiichi Ota

Editor
Mitsuzo Miyata

Script Girl
Yoshimi Kimura

Period Authenticity
Kusune Kainosho

Production Director
Masatsugu Hashimoto

Makeup
Zenya Fukuyama

Hairstyles
Ritsu Hanai

Still Photography
Ennosuke Asada

Locations
Daiei Studios in Kyoto and locations
 near Lake Biwa

Shooting Schedule
February 1953–March 1953

Process
Black and White

Negative
Fuji Film

Developing and Printing
Toyo Developing Co.

Release Date
March 23, 1953 (Japan)
August 1953 (Venice)

Length
97 minutes

Cast

Genjuro
Masayuki Mori

Miyagi
Kinuyo Tanaka

Genichi
Ichisaburo Sawamura

Tobei
Sakae Ozawa

Ohama
Mitsuko Mito

Lady Wakasa
Machiko Kyo

Ukon
Kikue Mori

Wakasa's Ladies-in-Waiting
Tokiko Mito
Tokuko Ueda

Headman
Ryosuke Kagawa

Commander
Eigoro Onoe

Commander's Retainer
Saburo Date

Lord Niwa
Kozabuno Ramon

Boatman
Ichiro Amano

Shopkeeper
Kichijiro Ueda

Old Buddhist Priest
Sugisaku Aoyama

Shinto Priest
Shozo Nanbu

Proprietress of the Brothel
Reiko Kondo

Prostitutes
Teruko Omi
Keiko Koyanagi
Masako Tomura

Soldiers
Jun Fujikawa
Ryuji Fukui
Eiji Ishiguro
Koji Fukuda

The Continuity Script

During the credits, No music is heard on the sound track. It is intermittently accentuated with koto music.

TITLE: Akinari Ueda's *Tales of Moonlight and Rain* offers readers stories rich in suggestions of mystery and fantasy. This film weaves a new spell from the illusions summoned up by his tales.

A Village on a Lake Shore, day

1. ELS: *the camera pans across a pastoral valley, showing tilled and un-tilled fields with scattered farmhouses and stands of trees.*

   TITLE: Kohoku in northern Omi province. It is early spring of the year, during the era of civil war.

   The camera continues panning over a small building, the kiln of a potter, and then reveals two houses at the edge of a village. The nearer dwelling belongs to Genjuro, the one in the background to Tobei, his younger brother-in-law.

   The camera cranes down and holds in LS on Genjuro, his wife Miyagi, and their small son, Genichi, in front of their house. The couple is busy loading bundles of pottery onto a two-wheeled cart. Genjuro begins to lash the bundles to the cart with rope. The sound-track music fades as gunshots are heard in the distance. They look up from their work in alarm. Miyagi picks up Genichi and holds him in her arms.

2. MS: *Genjuro and Miyagi on the far side of the cart.*

   MIYAGI: What is it?

   GENJURO: Probably Shibata's spies were captured and shot. (*Miyagi looks worried. Genjuro resumes tying the bundles to the cart.*) I must get to market before the battle begins. They say that business has been booming ever since Shibata's army came to town. (*Genjuro moves to the rear of the cart and tightens the straps on the bundles, his back now to the camera.*)

   MIYAGI: Can't I come along?

   GENJURO: No! Those ruthless foot soldiers are too dangerous. And anyway, you have to take care of our son, Genichi. You have to stay behind.

   Tobei and Ohama emerge from their house in the far background. Genjuro and Miyagi turn toward them because of the commotion they are making.

   OHAMA: Okay then. I can't stop you if you want to go so badly.

3. *Tobei puts on his hat and walks toward the camera into MS. Ohama follows.*

OHAMA: Run off and be a great samurai. Ha! I certainly won't mind if you manage to measure up.

TOBEI: (*stopping to look back toward Ohama*): Whoever succeeded without ambition? And any ambition worth having is big! Boundless, like the ocean! (*He walks on, leaving the frame at the right.*)

OHAMA (*moving forward into* MS): You don't even know how to hold a spear! And you think you'll be a great samurai?

4. LS: *pan follows Tobei and Ohama and holds in* LS *as they join Genjuro and Miyagi at the cart.*

OHAMA: Stick to what you know. Don't go running after bad luck.

TOBEI: You'll sing a different tune when I'm a success. I swear by the God of War, I'm sick and tired of being poor. (*To Genjuro.*) Brother, let me go with you!

GENJURO: Forget it! What a dumb idea!

TOBEI: I'll pull the cart. (*He moves to the front of the cart, steps between the shafts and begins to pull.*)

GENJURO: Don't be silly!

OHAMA: He's dreaming, brother. He thinks all he has to do is get to Nagahama to find fame and fortune waiting there for him.

GENJURO: It's no use talking sense to him. Miyagi, I'm leaving . . .

As the cart begins to move, Genjuro starts pushing it from behind. The men move out of the frame at the right, leaving the women in LS *looking after them.*

Dissolve.

A Mountain Road, day

5. MLS: *the camera cranes down as the cart advances toward it up a narrow path, with Tobei pulling hard and Genjuro pushing behind. They are hastening toward Nagahama in the northern part of the province. A villager passes in the other direction. The camera pans with the cart as it moves by, then holds as it moves away down the path.*

Fade out.

The Village, in Front of Genjuro's House, day

6. MLS: *the village headman is leaving the house, talking to Miyagi, who follows him respectfully with her child by her side.*

HEADMAN: What wild ambition! And Genjuro is just as bad as Tobei, really. I don't object to seizing an opportunity, but gains made in wartime have a way of vanishing into thin air. And it doesn't take much money to work up a greedy appetite.

7. ELS: *the headman pauses at the edge of the road, where his servant awaits him.*

HEADMAN: They'd be better off thinking how to prepare for the coming war. Tell Genjuro I said so when he returns. (*He and the servant start to leave, moving down the road, away from the camera.*)

MIYAGI: I will. Thank you for stopping by.

Miyagi bows and watches the headman leave. Turning to look down the road in the opposite direction, she reacts with a cry of delight to the sight of Genjuro, offscreen, coming back from Nagahama. The camera pans with her and Genichi, as they rush to greet him, then holds them in LS. *Genjuro puts down the shafts on the cart, reaches into his pouch, and takes out a handful of coins, thrusting them dramatically toward Miyagi.*

GENJURO: Look here!

8. MCU: *Genjuro proudly shows the coins to Miyagi.*

MIYAGI (*surprised*): Oh my! Where do you get all that?

GENJURO: Well, where do you suppose?

MIYAGI: But—so much profit!

GENJURO (*laughs*): Here! Feel how heavy. (*He puts the coins in her hands.*) I bet you've never laid eyes on so much money. I hurried back just to show you! (*Wipes his neck with a handkerchief.*) This is what real trading is all about. Now do you understand?

The camera tracks slowly after the family as they return to their house, holding them first in MS *and then in* LS.

MIYAGI: What about Tobei?

GENJURO: He came across a great samurai in Nagahama and went running after him. He wouldn't listen to me.

The Town of Nagahama, day

9. MLS: *the camera looks across a crowded street toward a large gateway from which many soldiers emerge. They are carrying supplies and military equipment to load on carts in the street. Tobei enters from the foreground, pauses with his back to the camera, and moves through the crowd toward the gate.*

10. LS: *Tobei is now seen from within the courtyard as he makes his way through the gate against the crowd of soldiers carrying supplies in the opposite direction. Tobei moves forward and leaves at screen right.*

11. LS: *Tobei crosses the courtyard, moving rapidly toward the camera. It tracks along with him as he rushes into an open, roofed building, deeply shadowed, where a number of soldiers are gathered. Now in* MS, *Tobei propels himself across the floor on his hands and knees, pushing past the legs of the soldiers until he can prostrate himself before the commander.*

TOBEI: Your lordship! Please take me into your service! I'll be a loyal retainer until my dying day.

SOLDIER: Since when do we make soldiers out of beggars?

COMMANDER (*putting on his armor, assisted by several soldiers*): If you really want to serve, you'll come dressed for the job.

His followers, shown only from the waist down as the camera holds on Tobei, kick and push the peasant off the edge of the floor out into the court-

yard. The camera tracks back as Tobei is pushed away, then tracks forward with him as he tries to reenter.

SOLDIER (*off*): Are you still hanging around? Where's your spear and armor? Get out of here, you filthy beggar!

Tobei, now in MS, *retreats, stunned by the rejection. The soldiers' laughter is heard offscreen.*

Dissolve.

Inside Genjuro's House, evening

12. MS: *Genjuro is sipping sake by the hearth. Behind him, Miyagi dresses Genichi in a new kimono and sends him to his father. Music starts on the sound track.*

MIYAGI: My! Isn't this lovely? Aren't you happy?

Genjuro cradles his son. Miyagi admires the new kimono that Genjuro brought her and tries it on. He looks very pleased.

MIYAGI: It's like New Year's and the Bon festival rolled into one.

Genjuro looks at her and laughs contentedly.

GENJURO: All these years, I've always wanted to buy you a new kimono. But I never could. At last my dream has come true! It makes me so happy to see you so pleased.

MIYAGI: Your kindness is what makes me happy, not the kimono. Really, I am satisfied just to be here all together. I don't yearn for money or anything else.

Still wrapped in her new kimono, Miyagi crosses behind Genjuro and begins to prepare dinner. Genjuro lifts a basket of goods that he brought from Nagayama.

GENJURO: Just think of it! Dried fish, oil, flour, sweet arrowroot, rice cakes—from our profits. (*He lifts another basket containing a bottle and places it beside him.*) With money we're happy. Without it, we suffer. It's hard to keep your hopes up with hardship dragging you down. So I'll work harder than ever. (*He begins to rise, carrying Genichi in his arms.*)

13. MLS: *the camera is behind Genjuro as he rises. It remains centered on Miyagi as Genjuro carries his son to the back of the room and surveys the pottery stored on the shelves.*

GENJURO: I can bring home even more money. I will make as much pottery as possible. (*Music ends. He sits on a bench below the shelves. Miyagi at the hearth has her back to him.*) That small batch fetched three silver coins.

MIYAGI: Please stop. We have enough money now. The headman says Lord Shibata's troops may come any day—maybe even tomorrow. We ought to be prepared, you here with us. (*Miyagi turns to face Genjuro.*)

GENJURO: How stupid can you be? War brings us prosperity. Didn't my
trip show that?

MIYAGI: Things could work out differently next time. (*Genjuro's smile
fades. He looks a bit surprised.*) Suppose something happened to
you . . .

GENJURO: You leave the worrying to me.

*He rises, putting Genichi down, as Ohama walks in the door. Genichi goes
to his mother.*

GENJURO: Say—Ohama!

OHAMA (*obviously worried about her husband*): Brother—

GENJURO: Now don't you fret. No self-respecting samurai will take on a
peasant dressed in rags. Tobei will return.

MIYAGI: Don't worry. he will be back soon. (*Ohama sits by the hearth.*)
Here, have some sake.

*As Miyagi offers sake to Ohama, a noise is heard outside. The camera
pans left with Ohama as she goes to the window: Tobei can be seen lurk-
ing outside the house. Ohama rushes out the door and the camera now
pans to the right as she pushes him inside. Tobei looks exhausted. Ohama
pushes him to the floor.*

OHAMA: You stupid idiot! I hope you've learned your lesson now. Just look
at you—a beggar! I hope you know you're the village laughingstock!

Fade out.

Genjuro's Workshop, day
Fade in.

14. MS: *Genjuro, in profile in the foreground, is throwing pots on his wheel. In the near background facing the camera, Miyagi turns the wheel. Their son enters and goes to Miyagi. Rhythmic beats are heard, synchronized to the motion of the potter's wheel.*

    GENJURO (*irritably*): Keep it moving.

    MIYAGI: Yes.

    GENJURO: Push him away! We're late as it is.

    MIYAGI (*to the child*): Be good and quiet, dear.

    GENICHI: Mama, I'm hungry.

    GENJURO: Why does he keep getting in the way?

    MIYAGI: You mustn't bother us now. I'll feed you soon.

    GENJURO: Just a few more turns, and we'll be finished.

    Miyagi pushes the child away.

15. MCU: *Miyagi looks solemn as she turns the wheel. Dissonant flute music, accentuated with a drum, starts on the sound track.*

    MIYAGI: You're completely changed. You're so grouchy. All I want is for us to work together happily—just the three of us. I don't care about anything else.

Genjuro's House, Outside the Kiln, day

16. L S : *Genjuro loads racks of pottery on trestles to dry in the sun. He moves toward the camera and picks up another rack from the ground.*

17. M L S : *Miyagi applies glaze to the dried pottery.*
    Dissolve.

18. L S : *Tobei, crouched outside the door of the kiln, hands pottery to Genjuro inside.*

    G E N J U R O : You really worked hard this time!

    T O B E I : That's because I'm still ambitious!

19. M C U : *Genjuro and Tobei continue to load the kiln. The camera focuses tightly on the door to the kiln.*

    G E N J U R O : When this batch is done, we'll go to Nagahama again. This time we'll strike it rich for sure.

    T O B E I : Do I get a share?

    G E N J U R O : Of course. I'll give you a third.

    T O B E I : I can't wait to see that money. I want to feel it warming in my hands.
    Dissolve.

Outside the Kiln, night

20. M L S : *high angle on Genjuro and Tobei asleep on a straw mat spread before the kiln.*

OHAMA (*off*): I have never seen Tobei and Genjuro work so hard before.
21. LS: *the camera looks across the sleeping men to where Miyagi and Ohama are feeding the kiln fire with wood.*
OHAMA: They've thrown themselves body and soul into this kiln. What would they do if they lost it all?
22. MS: *the two women continue working, Miyagi gathering sticks into bundles, Ohama feeding the fire.*
MIYAGI: All I ask is that the three of us live happily together. And yet Genjuro insists on taking this risk. Is that how men really are? Until now he has been so reliable. But war changes men!
OHAMA: Well . . . it would be nice to get some money ahead . . . (*Hearing some noises, she rises and moves toward the camera.*) What's that?
23. LS: *Ohama passes the sleeping men and moves into* MS; *in the background, Miyagi awakens her husband. Shouting and commotion can be heard in the village.*
MIYAGI: Wake up, dear! Please—get up!
The men rouse themselves. All four now look off screen right.
GENJURO: Must be Shibata's army.
Tobei dashes off screen right.
24. LS: *Tobei climbs a ladder to the top of an earthen rampart, from which he can survey the vicinity.*

25. ELS: *Tobei is on the rampart while Miyagi, Ohama, and Genjuro watch him from below.*
    GENJURO: Tobei, do you see anything?
    TOBEI: You bet! I can see the neighbors scattering like ants!
    MIYAGI: What shall we do?
    GENJURO: Well, we can't let the fire go out. We won't . . . I won't allow it. (*He stands by the kiln. Miyagi runs past him and off at screen left.*)
    TOBEI: They're coming to get us now.

26. CU: *a deep focus shot from inside Genjuro's house with Genichi sleeping in the foreground. Miyagi rushes into the house and runs toward her child.*
    MIYAGI (*shaking him*): Genichi!
    Now in CU, she picks him up, then turns and carries him out into the street.

27. MLS: *villagers flee their homes, carrying possessions.*

28. MLS: *a narrow street with more villagers rushing away from the camera and out of sight around a corner. Suddenly there is confusion and the villagers rush back the way they came; apparently they have met soldiers ahead of them. More soldiers now appear in the foreground and block their way.*
    SOLDIER: We'll take all the men. Surrender!

29. LS: *the camera looks down at Genjuro's house from just above the roof line of the kiln. Genjuro, Tobei, and Ohama are below in the foreground, next to the kiln. Miyagi stands across the way in front of the house, her child in her arms. Villagers rush past; some carry possessions while others push a wagon.*
    VILLAGER: Hurry! Run for your lives! Lord Shibata's army is coming!
    VILLAGER: Hide your rice and valuables!
    VILLAGER: Hide your women!
    VILLAGER: They'll take the men away with them! And all our food!

30. MLS: *Genjuro, Ohama, and Tobei watch. The camera follows as Genjuro dashes to his kiln.*
    GENJURO: What a pack of wolves! If only they'd come tomorrow, not tonight!
    Miyagi, carrying Genichi, runs to Genjuro.
    MIYAGI: Quick! We must go now! It's too dangerous.
    Genjuro is now firing the kiln. Tobei hesitates, then runs to the rampart ladder and climbs up.
    GENJURO: I could lose my fortune with this batch.
    MIYAGI: But you mustn't lose your life with it.

31. MCU: *Genjuro, in profile, continues to feed the fire.*
    GENJURO: Cook us some rice. We'll get ready to go to the mountain.

32. MS: *Miyagi and Ohama turn back toward the house, leaving in the foreground at screen left.*

A Street in the Village, night

33. MS: *the doorway of a house. Two women, screaming, run inside. They are pursued by two soldiers, who move more deliberately. Three other soldiers stay outside and watch through the doorway, laughing.*

Interior of a Peasant's House, night

34. MS: *the camera pans left in the dark interior as two villagers creep under straw to hide from approaching soldiers. Soldiers enter and find one man in hiding; they drag him away. Other soldiers discover the second villager.*
SOLDIER: Here they are.
The camera pans right and shoots through a doorway as the soldiers hustle their captives into the street. Two women follow the soldiers. One of them, clinging to a soldier in the street, pleads for her husband's life.
VILLAGE WOMAN: Please don't take my husband. Leave us our helper. Without him, we'll starve.
The soldier pushes the woman to the ground.

A Street in the Village, night

35. LS: *the camera looks out through a doorway as soldiers pass in the street, dragging villagers away. Ohama, carrying Genichi, stands beneath a gate.*
SOLDIER: Damn! He is hiding here.
VILLAGER: Please don't take me away!

36. MLS: *soldiers brutalize the villagers and plunder their homes. They push and drag their prisoners at spearpoint along a street and off frame right.*

A Mountain Road, night

37. MLS *(high angle): the villagers flee in moonlight through the woods. The camera cranes down and pans right as the villagers push carts and carry bundles of possessions on their backs.*

38. MS: *the camera track-pans parallel to lines of fleeing villagers as Genjuro leads Miyagi with Genichi on her back. Tobei and Ohama follow behind their neighbors. Ohama pushes her husband along as he keeps turning to look back. They disappear off screen left and other villagers file past.*
Dissolve.

By a Stream in the Mountains, night

39. MS: *the camera pans and tracks in on a group of villagers, who have stopped to rest by a stream. Other villagers cook food over a campfire. Genjuro, Genichi, and the two women are together in the background. Tobei is missing. Miyagi comes forward to receive a tray of rice from a villager and brings it back to her family. Genjuro holds Genichi. The camera pans to hold Genjuro's group in MS. Sounds of gunfire in the distance.*
MIYAGI: Let's eat while it's hot.
OHAMA *(noticing that her husband is missing)*: What has happened to Tobei?

GENJURO: That idiot!

The camera pans and follows Ohama as she crosses the stream to the path.

OHAMA (*to a villager*): Have you seen my husband?

VILLAGER: No.

Smoke from campfires billows in the foreground as Ohama walks along the path away from the camera, frame left, continuing her search.

In the Woods, night

40. MCU: *Tobei approaches the camera as he emerges from the woods. Drumbeats on the sound track. Stealthily, he crawls through undergrowth toward an encampment of soldiers. Sneaking up to the back of a hut, he attempts to steal body armor hanging from a rafter of the hut. A soldier hears the noise he makes.*

SOLDIER: Who goes there?

41. MLS: *in the foreground, the soldier comes running to investigate as Tobei hides under the hut. The soldier, finding no one, returns to the front of the hut. Again Tobei tries to steal the armor. This time, a soldier wakes from sleep with a loud yawn. Losing his nerve, Tobei runs off into the woods.*

By a Stream in the Mountains, night

42. MLS: *two villagers stand by a campfire, looking off into the distance.*

VILLAGER: It's pretty quiet now.

VILLAGER: Yeah. Not so much gunfire.

The camera shifts focus. Genjuro stands up in MCU in front of the camera. He looks off into the distance, gravely concerned. He starts to move off screen right.

43. MLS: *the village headman with another villager and Miyagi confront Genjuro.*

HEADMAN: Where do you think you're going? It's much too dangerous in the village. You'd be better off to relax and wait. The samurai will soon be gone.

VILLAGER: You have to wait.

GENJURO: I can't wait a moment longer! I've got to go!

Ignoring their advice, he starts to leave again. The camera pans with him as Miyagi follows, pulling at his arm.

MIYAGI: Stop him!

GENJURO: If that fire dies down, we'll lose everything!

With Genichi on her back, Miyagi struggles to prevent her husband from returning to the kiln.

MIYAGI: Genjuro, please give up the kiln. If Shibata's soldiers catch you, they'll make you a coolie. (*Miyagi sets the child down and clutches Genjuro.*) We can always make new pottery.

GENJURO: No, we can't. I won't let those be ruined!

Genjuro breaks free and runs off screen left into the woods. Miyagi places Genichi in Ohama's care and then also runs off screen left.

Genjuro's Kiln, night

44. ELS (*high angle*): *a steep path near the kiln. The camera tilts down as Genjuro runs along toward the kiln. The camera cranes down into* MLS *and follows him around the building until he reaches the kiln and peers inside.*

GENJURO: Oh, no! The fire's gone out!

The camera pans left with Genjuro as he inspects the cold oven. In the background, Miyagi comes running along the path toward the camera.

MIYAGI (*anxiously*): Genjuro!

GENJURO: Oh God! It's out cold.

Miyagi looks into the kiln. Genjuro hears the noise of approaching soldiers. He grabs Miyagi and pulls her away.

45. LS: *Genjuro's house from in front of the kiln. Gunshots are heard. As Genjuro and Miyagi disappear from the foreground, several soldiers, armed with spears, emerge from Genjuro's house. They smash a large vase on the ground and approach the kiln.*

SOLDIER 1: Hey, look here!

SOLDIER 2: Maybe one of them is hiding in here.

SOLDIER 3: They must have hidden something inside.

SOLDIER 4: We'll see.

Two soldiers use a post to break into the kiln. Using a torch for light, they peer inside.

SOLDIER 1: Damn! Nothing but pots! Let's get out of here.

Disappointed, the soldiers move on. Another group of soldiers appears from behind the kiln, leading some captives away.

SOLDIER: Hey, get moving!

46. MS: *Genjuro emerges from his hiding place behind the kiln. The camera tracks with him as he pulls out a piece of pottery and discovers that it is fired. Miyagi peers over his shoulder.*

GENJURO: They did get fired! Look! They're ready!

MIYAGI: Are they really all right?

The camera tracks in as they start to unload the kiln, surprised to find their wares in such good shape.

47. MS: *Tobei arrives with Ohama carrying Genichi. Everyone is excited.*

GENJURO: They're all just fine! Thank God!

TOBEI (*as Miyagi takes Genichi from Ohama*): Fired? Does that mean we go back to Nagahama?

GENJURO: This time, we'll take a boat across the lake.

TOBEI: Ohama is a fisherman's daughter. She can row us.

OHAMA: How do we get to the lake from here?

GENJURO: We'll take a short cut.

TOBEI: Can we find any boat?

GENJURO: Surely we'll find a boat left behind. Let's hurry and unload the kiln.

Genjuro puts on gloves and starts emptying the kiln. They all work quickly. Dissolve.

Lake Biwa, Onoe Beach, night

48. ELS: *a boat is beached on the shore. Drumbeats begin. Gunfire is again heard in the distance. Genjuro, Miyagi, Tobei, and Ohama hurry to load their merchandise into the boat. Genichi sits in the middle. The others get in. Tobei pushes off and they are afloat.*

Fade out.

On the Lake, night

Fade in.

49. LS: *thick mist hovers over the calm water of the lake. Slowly, the ghostly image of the prow of a boat appears through the fog. Someone stands upright, working a single oar. It is Ohama, singing as she rows. As the boat approaches the camera, its image clarifies. We see the occupants.*

50. MCU: *Genjuro and Tobei, leaning against the parcels in the middle of the boat, drink sake. The camera pans laterally to show Miyagi, who is holding Genichi and gazing off into the mist.*

GENJURO: Be careful! The fog is really thick.

MIYAGI (*to Genichi*): Look, Genichi. This is the lake. Isn't it pretty?

GENJURO: We're safe at last.

The camera pulls back as Ohama continues to work the oar.

MIYAGI: What a good idea to go by water! On land, we might have been killed.

The camera pans left and holds Genjuro, Tobei, and Miyagi in MLS.

TOBEI: We should reach Omizo by daybreak. Lord Gorozaemon Niwa has his castle there. It's even more of a boom-town than Nagahama.

GENJURO: Tobei, this time we'll really strike it rich. Our wives will be rich too! I'll put up a big warehouse right in our village!

The boat rocks gently as the men continue to drink sake.

TOBEI: I'll buy myself a suit of armor!

Miyagi and Genichi silently nibble on rice cakes.

51.   MS *(high angle): Ohama continues to row, pulling strongly on the oar, singing softly. She abruptly stops singing and turns to gaze into the fog. The drumbeats grow louder.*

52.   LS: *another boat emerges from the fog, drifting aimlessly toward them. It appears to be empty.*

53.   LS: *the unknown boat drifts nearer, moving to the right, with the prow of Genjuro's boat visible at the right.*

TOBEI: Hey, look! A boat!

From frame right, Tobei uses a hook to draw the other boat alongside. Everyone looks into it.

MIYAGI: Oh, a ghost!

54.   CU *(high angle): an injured man is lying face down in the boat.*

MAN: No, no! Don't think I'm a ghost. (*He lifts his head.*) I am a boat-man from Kaizu. I was attacked by pirates . . . on my way . . . to Azuchi!

55.   MCU: *Tobei and Genjuro stare at the wounded man, the back of whose head is visible in the foreground.*

MAN: Water . . . give me water . . .

Genjuro, quaking, pours sake into a bowl and hands it to the man.

MAN: Thank you! (*He takes the cup and drinks with trembling hands.*)

56.   MCU: *Miyagi clutches Genichi as Ohama kneels. They are visibly shaken.*

MAN *(off):* I don't know where you're going. But watch out for pirates.

57.   MCU: *as in shot 55. Tobei and Genjuro listen intently to the wounded man.*

MAN: When they catch you, they will take your cargo, and your life. Women they take with them. Beware . . .

The man rolls over on his back . . .

58.   MS *(high angle): . . . and expires. The camera looks across the dead man's boat toward Genjuro's. Ohama folds her hands and prays for the repose of the dead man's soul, reciting the name of Amida Buddha. Tobei pushes the other boat away from them. Ohama finishes her prayer. Miyagi gazes after the dead man's boat as it drifts away.*

MIYAGI: *(to Genjuro)*: Let's go back. This is an omen. We mustn't go on.
GENJURO *(standing)*: You women will be safer ashore. We'll go on by ourselves, trusting to heaven.
MIYAGI: No! Please don't!
OHAMA: Tobei, I'm going with you. I don't trust you out of my sight.
TOBEI: But they take women . . .
OHAMA: We'll see about that. I'm coming along.
Tobei stands and begins to pole.
MIYAGI: I'm coming too. Genjuro, please!
GENJURO: You have to take care of Genichi. Ohama, turn us around!
MIYAGI: Genjuro, please let me go with you!
Miyagi continues to plead as the boat changes course. Tobei leans on his pole at the front of the boat and Ohama takes up her oar at the rear again. As Ohama works her oar, the boat turns away from the camera and vanishes in the fog.
Dissolve.

59. MLS: *Miyagi and Genichi are standing on the shore. The boat is in the foreground. It is moving to the left with Genjuro, Tobei, and Ohama aboard. The camera tracks left as Miyagi and Genichi walk on the shore parallel to the boat.*
GENJURO *(calling to Miyagi)*: As soon as I get the money I'll be back. In less than ten days. Just wait.

60. MCU: *the camera tracks Miyagi and Genichi as they follow the progress of the departing boat.*
MIYAGI: Heaven protect you! If you meet any pirates, don't try to fight them off.

61. MCU *(reverse angle track)*: *Genjuro and Ohama are organizing the load of pottery in the boat. Genjuro calls to Miyagi from the boat.*
GENJURO: Okay, okay. You stay off the main road. Take the long way back through the mountains. And stay clear of our house. I know it will be hard, but try to be patient. I'll try not to be long.

62. CU *(reverse angle)*: *Miyagi nods sadly and picks up Genichi in her arms.*
MIYAGI: Tobei! Ohama! Take care of yourselves! And of my husband!

63. MLS *(camera still tracking)*: *Genjuro and Ohama call to Miyagi from the boat as Tobei poles.*
OHAMA: Don't worry. Just wait for us. We'll be back soon.
GENJURO: We'll be back before you know. Take good care of Genichi. *(The boat moves off frame left as Miyagi and Genichi come to the edge of the shore.)* I'll come back with a heap of silver coins.
Genichi waves. His farewell to his father is heard on the sound track.

64. MCU: *with tears in her eyes Miyagi stands on the shore, holding Genichi and watching the boat move out onto the lake.*
MIYAGI: Good luck! And be careful!

The camera dollies left with Miyagi and Genichi as they follow along the shoreline. Miyagi takes Genichi on her back. Genichi keeps calling to his father. The drumbeats end.
Fade out.

Omizo Castletown, day
Fade in.

65. LS: *overhead shot of a busy marketplace. People mill around, buying and selling, loitering and arguing. A juggler performs in the midst of all this frenetic activity. The camera pans left, cranes down, and tracks through the crowd toward Genjuro, Tobei, and Ohama, selling their pottery.*

66. MS *(high angle): Genjuro, sitting, offers a bowl for sale as customers gather in front of the pottery stand. The camera tracks back and right to include Tobei collecting money from a sale. Beside him, Ohama busily unpacks more merchandise.*

67. LS *(high angle): a woman, dressed in an elegant kimono and wearing a wide-brimmed traveling hat, approaches the pottery stand from the rear, accompanied by another woman who stands behind her.*

68. MS *(high angle): the woman, looking down at Genjuro, points to some items.*

WOMAN: I'll have that vase.

GENJURO: This one?

WOMAN: That sake bottle, too. And that cup and those bowls.

Genjuro collects the items together and turns toward the woman. He looks intently at her face, his expression registering surprise.

69. MS (*reverse low angle*): *the woman, with her face visible for the first time. Her face is made up like that of a female No mask. The lady's attendant, an older woman, steps forward and points to other items.*

OLD WOMAN: And those rice bowls, too, and plates. Also those pots. (*Genjuro turns and repeats the order.*) We live in the Kutsuki mansion near the mountain. Do you deliver? We'll pay you then.

GENJURO (*bobbing nervously, speaking in a choked voice, his eyes fixed on the young woman*): Thank you very much . . . thank you, ma'am.

The two women turn and leave as Genjuro stands and stares after them. Courtly music grows louder.

70. MLS: *soldiers come running past the stand, shouting above the noise.*

SOLDIER: Inspector from the castle will pass! Clear the way! His lordship is coming!

The crowd clears the way. The camera tracks back. In the turmoil, Genjuro stands still, staring after the two women. Then he crouches down with Tobei and Ohama, out of the way. The inspector on horseback gallops through, followed by a retinue on foot. Tobei looks up at them yearningly. Ohama notices and pulls at his sleeve, trying to block his view.

OHAMA (*to Tobei*): Look away! Don't you dare gawk at them! You'll get caught up in those idiotic dreams of yours all over again.

Tobei is awestruck. He steps toward the camera into MS, *straining for a better view.*

71. LS: *the camera looks through an alleyway (from Tobei's point of view) as he watches Lord Niwa's party pass down another street.*

72. MS: *Tobei, as at the end of 70. He moves forward into* MCU, *still staring after the horsemen.*

TOBEI: All I need is a suit of armor . . . then I could be a samurai too! And a sword and spear.

Tobei holds up a small pouch that hangs on a thong around his neck. The camera tracks as Ohama rushes up to him. Fast drumbeats begin on the soundtrack.

OHAMA: Give me that pouch. It's our hard-earned money. Don't even think of throwing it away on such a foolish dream! (*To Genjuro.*) Stop him, brother!

Genjuro comes running as she tries to snatch the pouch. The three of them grapple.

TOBEI: Please! I'll come back. I'll be a great samurai!

OHAMA: Oh, stop him, brother! Tobei, Tobei . . .

Genjuro, distracted by customers, runs back to the stand. The camera pans left as Ohama runs to grab Genjuro, who hesitates because of the customers. The camera then pans right as she runs back to where Tobei was, but now he has vanished in the crowd. Ohama chases after him.

An Armorer's, day

73. MS: *the camera, positioned inside an armorer's shop, looks out onto the street. In the foreground, we see the armorer making his wares while people pass in the background. Tobei rushes by, looking for a place to hide. Ohama runs past, calling to her husband, then goes in a different direction. Moments later, Tobei returns, sees that his wife has left, and enters the shop.*

ARMORER (*surprised at the commotion he has seen*): What's the matter? *Tobei looks at a suit of armor.*

TOBEI (*displaying the moneypouch*): I'll have a suit of armor!

Nearby, day

74. MLS (*high angle*): *a crowded street. Ohama appears, running toward the camera. She pauses, calls out for Tobei, and the camera pans with her as she runs off frame right.*

An Armorer's, day

75. MCU: *Tobei is being fitted with a piece of chest armor by the armorer.*

TOBEI (*laughing and stepping back*): How do you like that? Do I look just like a samurai?

ARMORER: Like a great warrior. But you must carry a spear.

TOBEI: Then get me one!

ARMORER: Here you are.

He hands a spear to Tobei, who arrogantly thrusts it at a display of armor, knocking it over, much to the displeasure of the armorer.

TOBEI: How much? Here's a silver coin.

Tobei pays the armorer. Drumbeats end.

Dissolve.

Near a Temple Along a Road in the Countryside, evening

76. LS: *Ohama, walking along a deserted path, pauses to rest on a bench at the edge of a lake. Insects are chirping. Suddenly, a group of soldiers with grins on their faces appear at frame left immediately behind her. The camera cranes up as they surround her. Ohama tries to run away along the lake shore, but the soldiers grab her and force her to the ground. She throws dirt at them and breaks free.*

77. LS (*high angle*): *the soldiers catch Ohama in some underbrush.*

OHAMA: What are you going to do? Help! Help!

The soldiers pin Ohama to the ground, gag her, then lift her on their shoulders and carry her into a temple, as the camera pans left to follow them.

Inside the Temple, evening

78. MCU: *the soldiers set Ohama on the temple floor, in front of the camera. She attempts to crawl away. Realizing that she is trapped, she moans and turns away. Two soldiers crouch over her.*

The Road outside the Temple, evening

79. CU: *Ohama's sandals, left by the edge of a lake.*

Outside the Temple, evening

80. LS: *soldiers sit in a small circle and patiently wait their turn in front of the temple. On the sound track, the No chorus, accentuated by the drum-beat, is introduced. One of the soldiers in the group stands up, facing the temple.*

Inside the Temple, evening

81. CU: *a soldier's hand as he reaches into his moneypouch, throws some coins on the floor next to Ohama, and leaves. She lies in a spot of light in* MS, *writhing in agony.*

Outside the Temple, evening

82. LS: *the soldiers leave the porch of the temple. Ohama staggers out to the porch. Her back is shown in silhouette to the camera as she descends the steps and pauses in front of the temple.*

83. MS: *Ohama, dishevelled and miserable, leans against a post at the foot of the temple porch and shouts out loud to her missing husband.*

OHAMA: You stupid idiot! Look at me now! I hope you're satisfied to see your wife used in such a way! (*The No chorus ends, but the drum-beat continues.*) You'd probably not even notice, you're so happy being a samurai. Tobei, you're a fool! (*She runs back up the steps and collapses, sobbing, on the temple porch, her back to the camera. The drum-beat ends.*)

Fade out.

Omizo Castletown, evening

Fade in.

84. MS: *most of the crowd has left the marketplace, and vendors are closing up shop. A wandering musician strolls by. Genjuro, alone, is packing his wares. Flute music begins.*

GENJURO (*to a neighbor*): Will you keep an eye on my pottery until my partner returns?

NEIGHBOR: Surely.

Genjuro leaves, carrying packages to deliver to the Kutsuki mansion.

85. MLS: *with his parcels, Genjuro walks along a street toward the camera and pauses in front of a kimono shop.*

86. MS: *the street as seen from inside the shop. In the left foreground, a tailor is sewing. Genjuro approaches the shop at center screen.*

87. MS: *pan (from Genjuro's point of view) shows the beautiful clothes on display in the shop. The flute music is still heard on the sound track.*

88. MS: *as in 86. The shopkeeper ignores Genjuro.*
     GENJURO: How much is this?
     SHOPKEEPER (*looking up*): You interested?
     GENJURO (*sitting down just outside the shop*): I might be. But how much?
     SHOPKEEPER (*giving a disdainful laugh*): It's not exactly something for
       your wife.
89. MCU: *Genjuro seen from inside the shop and framed by the hanging
     fabrics.*
     GENJURO: I can afford it. (*He smiles and hefts a pouch full of coins.*)
     Music ends.
90. CU: *the camera, from Genjuro's point of view, focuses on a particular
     kimono. Lyrical music, featuring harp and strings, begins.*
91. MCU: *as in 89. Genjuro pauses, looking at a kimono, as if in some
     reverie.*
92. MLS: *in Genjuro's vision, Miyagi appears in silhouette through the back
     door of the shop, carrying a tray of pottery. She puts down the tray and
     comes forward to where the kimonos are displayed. The camera tracks
     back to hold her in MS over Genjuro's shoulder. She admires the kimonos
     and wraps one around her shoulders as Genjuro watches. Then she drops
     the kimono and leaves.*
93. MCU: *the music fades as Genjuro recovers from his reverie. A voice calls
     to get his attention.*
     OLD WOMAN (*off*): Excuse me.
     Genjuro turns.
94. MLS: *the elegant woman and her attendant seen from Genjuro's point of
     view. The old woman approaches him.*
     OLD WOMAN: We thought you might need help finding your way to us.
95. MCU: *Genjuro.*
     GENJURO (*rising and bowing humbly*): Thank you. You are very kind.
96. CU: *the camera looks into the face of the beautiful woman. Her face, with
     its resemblance to a female No mask, has a mysterious aura.*
97. MS: *the two women facing Genjuro, the beautiful woman in the
     foreground with her back to the camera.*
     OLD WOMAN: Come along, then.
     *The women turn and Genjuro follows, all moving toward the camera.
     Drumbeats are heard on the sound track.
     Dissolve.*
     A Road through the Mountains, evening
98. LS: *the camera pans right as Genjuro follows the women along a lake
     shore and through a marsh. Bolero music begins on the sound track.*
     The Kutsuki Mansion, night
99. MLS: *the gate to the mansion, seen from inside the garden, is open and
     unattended. It swings eerily in the breeze. The shadows of the women*

ripple across a neglected and weed-choked garden . The camera pans with the women as they continue through the overgrown garden, followed by Genjuro.

100. MS: *the shadows of the three distinctly fall against the wall of the mansion as they pass by.*

101. MS: *the camera track-pans right as the lady and her old attendant approach and enter the house. The camera holds in LS as Genjuro, following meekly, stops and waits outside. The attendant returns to the door.*

    OLD WOMAN: Please come in.

    GENJURO: Yes, but guess I'd better be on my way . . .

102. MS *(low angle): Genjuro sets his parcels on the porch and bows to the attendant, who is facing the camera. They are in semi-darkness.*

    OLD WOMAN: Lady Wakasa is expecting you. Come in.

    GENJURO: Do you mean that young lady?

    OLD WOMAN: Yes, she is the only surviving child of Lord Saemon Kutsuki. Do come in. You're quite welcome.

    Genjuro follows the attendant inside.

103. LS: *the camera cranes down and pans in a long sweep, following as the old attendant leads Genjuro along the dark corridor. The bare trees of the courtyard are bathed in moonlight. Arriving at the entryway to the main room, under the boughs of a pine tree, Genjuro hands the parcels to the attendant.*

    OLD WOMAN: Thank you for your trouble. Please come in.

    Genjuro bows several times.

    OLD WOMAN: Please come in.

    Genjuro kneels at the side of the entrance.

104. MCU *(low angle): Genjuro waits. In the background, the old attendant is a black silhouette as she glides into a room. Genjuro turns. Illuminated by the moonlight, he stares into the courtyard.*

105. MLS: *the mansion as seen from the courtyard. Other ladies-in-waiting appear and light the lamps one after another in the rooms along the corridor. A warm glow envelops the house, as if it had come to life.*

106. MCU: *curious, Genjuro looks around as the room becomes brighter. He seems astonished by its elegance.*

107. MS: *a single candle illuminates a room with a screen painting of two cranes in the background. Emerging as a shadowy figure, Lady Wakasa enters the room at frame left and smiles. The camera pans to hold her in MCU as she walks into the light of the main room. No music begins on the sound track.*

108. MS: *Lady Wakasa approaches Genjuro, who is still on his knees. She kneels, and gently takes him by the hand. They rise and she leads him into the main room.*

    LADY WAKASA: Please. You are Genjuro of Northern Omi, aren't you?

They sit on a mat in the center of the room and are served by attendants. The camera slowly dollies in.

GENJURO: How did you happen to know my name, ma'am?

LADY WAKASA: When I caught sight of your wares in that crowded market, I could scarcely believe my own eyes. (*Genjuro bows humbly.*) Your blue glaze had such a pearly sheen. My father taught me how to appreciate the rare and beautiful. (*She rises and begins to circle behind Genjuro.*)

109. MCU *(high angle)*: *Lady Wakasa circles and kneels beside Genjuro. Her figure is bathed in light and we see only the shadowy back of Genjuro, whose head remains bowed.*

LADY WAKASA: I just had to see you in person and ask how you manage to create such beauty. But of course you have your secret formulas, never to be revealed.

GENJURO: Oh no, ma'am. There is no secret but hard work preparing clay and glazes. But glazing depends on the way you knead. There may be a knack you acquire through years of practice. It's not something that can be taught, exactly.

LADY WAKASA: Spoken like a true craftsman devoted to his art! But still, it takes a master's gift to create such exquisite beauty!

A bell chimes on the sound track. During the shots 110–112, the bell is heard intermittently,

110. MCU *(low angle)*: *the old woman, followed by attendants, enters with trays of food and sake, which have been arranged in Genjuro's ceramic ware. They kneel and place the trays before Genjuro.*

GENJURO: Well, I'll be! Aren't these my things?

The camera dollies in on Genjuro with Lady Wakasa at his side. Astonished, he examines the bowls.

LADY WAKASA: Yes. I want to use all your beautiful creations to have sake.

GENJURO (*talking to the bowls*): You are so lucky, my little ones, to be noticed by such a noble lady! So these are the pieces made by the peasant in his spare time. But you know I always think of my creations as my children. And now to see them honored by the touch of you, my lady . . . and in a house as fine as this! I would never have dared to dream of it! (*He bows deeply as another bowl is passed to Lady Wakasa.*)

LADY WAKASA: I'm sorry to say I fear for your little masterpieces. They may be spoiled by the touch of one so lowly as I. Please, have some sake. (*She offers sake to Genjuro.*)

111. MCU: *Genjuro, in profile, accepts a bowl of sake, his eyes fixed on the creation in his hand. In the background, Lady Wakasa, fully lit, pours as she faces the camera. In the foreground at frame left, we see the shadowy figure of the old woman, her back to the camera.*

GENJURO: It never occurred to me that my work could look so beautiful! (*When Genjuro drinks a chime is heard.*) I am surprised that things could gain so much beauty from their surroundings. But I feel awkward and strange, seeing my wares being used by you. (*He returns the cup to Lady Wakasa, takes the sake bottle, and offers her sake.*)

LADY WAKASA: Craftsmanship like yours must not lie buried in a poor village. You must try to refine your talent.

GENJURO: But what do you advise?

112. MS (*reverse angle*): *the old woman.*

OLD WOMAN: Take Lady Wakasa's advice! Now is your opportunity! Wed her at once!

The old woman leaves. The camera pulls back as Genjuro turns to face Lady Wakasa. She stands up, her back to the camera, and approaches Gen-

juro. As he stands, she throws her arms around him. No music begins.
They embrace and sink to the floor.

113. CU (*high angle*): *Lady Wakasa smiles, then breaks away from Genjuro.*

114. MS: *as Lady Wakasa runs from the room, her attendants enter. They take Genjuro's arms and lift him to his feet. The music ends.*

115. MS: *the camera shows the shadows of Genjuro and the attendants behind a screen, as he removes his old kimono. Biwa music begins on the sound track.*
Dissolve.

116. LS (*high angle*): *the courtyard shrouded in mist, the warm glow of the house in the background. Lady Wakasa is heard singing.*

     LADY WAKASA (*song*): The finest silk, of rarest shade . . .

117. MCU: *Lady Wakasa in profile hums softly, and starts to dance with great elegance. As the camera pans to follow her, Genjuro can be seen in the background, now dressed as handsomely as Lady Wakasa. He sips sake and watches.*

     LADY WAKASA (*song*): . . . may fade away, and quickly, too. So may the love I offer you . . .

118. CU: *Lady Wakasa continues to sing.*

     LADY WAKASA (*song*): . . . if your heart proves false to me.
     An ethereal male voice becomes audible, singing in counterpoint to Lady Wakasa. Wakasa's song fades. She stops singing, shaken. The light in the

room goes dark. The male voice continues to sing as the camera pans to
reveal in C U a military helmet in an alcove.
119. M C U : *Lady Wakasa is in shadowed profile in the foreground with light on
her old attendant in the background. The ethereal voice grows louder.*
OLD WOMAN : How pleased that voice sounds!
*The camera pans as Lady Wakasa rushes to Genjuro fearfully and
embraces him.*
LADY WAKASA : Do you hear that music? The man's voice is the voice
of my late father.
120. C U : *the helmet, supported on a figurine.*
121. M C U : *the old attendant. The camera pulls back as she stands, and, holding a musical instrument, approaches Genjuro and Lady Wakasa. She
kneels before them. The camera holds over Genjuro's shoulder.*
OLD WOMAN : The entire Kutsuki clan fell victim to that terrible
Nobunaga Oda. Only this young lady survived with her old nurse. And I
am that old woman, Ukon. His lordship's spirit still dwells with us in
this house. And when Her Ladyship dances, he sings like this. (*The
music merges with the man's song. The drum beats more quickly.*) Isn't
it a wonderful voice? Now it expresses his joy, since Her Ladyship is
going to wed.
Genjuro is overwhelmed. He turns and moves away. The camera pulls back.
LADY WAKASA : Whenever I hear his voice . . .
*Lady Wakasa moves to Genjuro and embraces him. The music ends.
Dissolve.*
122. M S : *Harp music begins on the sound track. Genjuro is asleep in a
bedroom as Lady Wakasa, who has been lying next to him, arises, gazes
lovingly at him, and moves to her mirror. She kneels before the mirror and
brushes her hair.*
123. M C U : *Genjuro sleeping. Lady Wakasa enters in the background and
kneels beside Genjuro. She pulls a lantern closer and gazes at his face.
Genjuro awakens and sits up.*
LADY WAKASA : It's much too early to get up. Stay in bed.
GENJURO : What I am doing here?
LADY WAKASA (*laughing coyly*): Why are you talking like this? (*She
turns her head modestly.*) As if you had forgotten everything.
UKON (*off*): Is His Lordship awake now?
Genjuro turns.
124. M S : *Ukon kneels in the foreground shadow.*
UKON : Take your beloved husband to the spring and bathe him, my lady.
I won't intrude.
*Ukon chuckles and the camera pans left with her as she leaves the room.
Lady Wakasa stands, Genjuro kneels. The pan continues into a wipe reveal-
ing the moonlit foliage of the next scene.*

The Hot Spring among the Rocks, night

125. MLS: *the camera pans left through the leafy trees to reveal a natural hot-spring pool. Birds are chirping. The camera holds in* LS, *showing Genjuro soaking as Lady Wasaka approaches, kneels, and washes his back. Music begins.*

    LADY WAKASA (*laughing coquettishly*): You don't trust me. You think I'm an evil women, don't you?

126. MS: *she washes Genjuro's back. He turns and clasps her hands. She stands and bends over to look into Genjuro's face, stroking his hand.*

    LADY WAKASA: But you have become mine, all mine. From now on, you belong to me, body and soul.

    The camera pans right as she moves away behind the bushes. She begins to disrobe as she leaves the frame at right. Two types of music—eerie and lyrical—merge.

127. MCU: *Genjuro watches Lady Wasaka's off-screen movements with anticipation. We hear her giggle as Genjuro moves toward her. Then water splashes over the edge as she enters the water, still off-screen. The camera tracks and pans left, following the water as it flows down the side of the pool and over rocks and stones below. The pan merges with an overhead shot of raked ground reminiscent of a Zen garden. There is a very slow dissolve as the camera movement overlaps into the next shot.*

A Lawn, day

128. ELS: *the camera pans and tilts up to reveal a bright sunny day. High angle shot of Lady Wakasa and Genjuro as they picnic next to two leafless trees along a lake shore with distant mountains in the background. They are seated on a picnic blanket spread on the grass, which stretches far away around them. Sake and food are placed in front of Genjuro. Wakasa sings, beating a drum. Genjuro moves close to her but she slips away. As Genjuro chases her, she eludes him, tauntingly. Music begins.*

129. MCU *(low angle)*: *they run toward the camera. Genjuro catches Lady Wakasa and embraces her.*

GENJURO: What do I care if you were a ghost or an evil spirit? I will never let you go, my lady. I never dreamed that there could be pleasure like this in life!

The camera pans right as Lady Wakasa escapes his embrace, but he drunkenly attempts to follow her. She eludes him as he falls, struggles to his feet, and falls again.

130. MCU: *Genjuro is on the ground, writhing in pleasure. The camera moves into CU as Lady Wakasa embraces him, rubbing her face on his.*

GENJURO: I must be in heaven! This must be paradise!

Music ends.

A Poor Farmer's Dwelling, evening

131. CU: *in the darkness of a farmhouse, Miyagi and Genichi are hiding from looting soldiers. She hears screams and peers out the window. Clutching*

Genichi, she slinks into a corner as soldiers walk by. The camera follows in M S *as she moves to another corner. The camera continues to pan left to look into the next room, the kitchen, as soldiers enter, looking for food.*

SOLDIER: Is there any food?

Finding no food, the soldiers leave. An old woman, carrying a kettle, sneaks inside and scuttles across the lower foreground. The camera pans right with her as she moves into the corner where Miyagi is hiding.

OLD WOMAN: Quick! Get hold of yourself!

132. MCU *(low angle): in another house, starving soldiers find food. They quickly eat everything they find.*

133. MCU: *outside, the camera pans slightly left as the old woman emerges from the back of the house, peers down the road heading away from the camera, then turns back to beckon Miyagi, who joins her in* MCU.

OLD WOMAN: Come! Quick! Take this food with you. (*She stuffs the food inside the front of Miyagi's kimono and then presses her hands.*)

MIYAGI: I'll never forget your kindness.

OLD WOMAN: You will be safe if you escape by the back road. Be sure to take the back road. To the left. Take care!

Miyagi runs down the moonlit road away from the camera with Genichi on her back.

134. MS: *in another house, a woman screams as soldiers break in, looting and fighting among themselves over the spoils.*

Fade out.

A Mountain Road, daybreak

Fade in.

135. ELS *(high angle): Miyagi is carrying Genichi along a road. She is stopped by two soldiers stepping out of a hut.*

SOLDIER: Have you got any food?

The ravenous soldiers reach into her bundle and grab the food. It falls to the ground. A third soldier, carrying a spear, joins in the struggle for the food.

MIYAGI: This food is for my boy! I beg you not to take it!

The camera moves in to MLS. *Each soldier scrambles for the rice cakes. Miyagi tries to defend herself, still with Genichi clinging to her back. One soldier, obviously dazed with hunger, thrusts his spear into her. She falls to the ground. Genichi cries.* MS *shows her rise, aided by a stick, still struggling to carry her child away from danger. In the background the soldiers devour the rice cakes. Miyagi collapses and tries to crawl away.*

Fade out.

A Marsh, day

Fade in.

136. MS: *the camera pans as a soldier carries his wounded commander through the reeds to safety. Shouts and gunfire are heard in the distance throughout the scene.*

137. MCU: *the camera tracks ahead of Tobei who is moving through tall grass, spear in hand. He moves past the camera, which then pans to follow him in* LS. *We then see that Tobei is pursuing the wounded man, who has halted outside a temple.*

138. CU: *Tobei crawls through the grass toward the camera. It tracks ahead of him, then holds him in* ECU.

139. LS (*high angle*): *outside the temple, the wounded commander prepares to commit suicide. Tobei hides under the porch of the temple frame left and watches.*

    COMMANDER: Be brave and do your duty!

    The commander kneels behind a rock, out of view of the camera. His retainer, who is still visible, draws a sword and beheads the commander, as instructed. Then, grief-stricken by the loss of his master, he wraps the severed head in a cloth. The camera cranes up and pulls back to reveal the body of the commander. Tobei comes from behind and stabs the soldier with his spear, then stabs the fallen soldier twice in the chest. Noticing the wrapped head, he steals it and runs away.
    Dissolve.

    Lord Niwa's Army Encampment, day

140. ELS: *in the midst of a throng of soldiers, Tobei runs along the street to Lord Niwa's headquarters.*

    TOBEI (*shouting*): I am here to report that I have taken an enemy commander's head!

141. MS (*low angle*): *Tobei in the foreground, his back to the camera, kneels on the porch of Lord Niwa's headquarters. Above him, in the background, Lord Niwa, eating a meal, pauses as Tobei offers the wrapped head to a retainer. The soldier places the head in front of Lord Niwa.*

    TOBEI: Look! Look at this!

    A retainer unwraps the cloth and steps aside.

    LORD NIWA: You have found a chieftain's head!

    TOBEI: No, sir, this is not luck! I really stabbed him with my spear!

142. MS (*reverse angle*): *Tobei, timidly drawing nearer Lord Niwa.*

    LORD NIWA: Ha, ha! Do you know who he is? The distinguished Katsushige Fuwa. He served Yasumasa Sakuma. How could such a famous fighter be slain by a foot soldier like you? This may be a find, but you should get a reward for it. What do you want?

    Lord Niwa stands as the camera pulls back into LS. *Soldiers have gathered round to witness this event.*

    TOBEI: Thank you, sir. I would like a horse, a suit of armor, and ten men. (*Trembling, Tobei bows low in profile to Lord Niwa.*)

    LORD NIWA: Very well! You shall have them.

    TOBEI: Thank you, thank you, sir.

    LORD NIWA: Your demand pleases me.

Tobei, startled, jumps back and bows low on the ground.
Fade out.

Omizo Castletown, evening

Fade in.

143.   L S (*high angle*): *Tobei, dressed in armor and proudly mounted, leads a band of retainers along a crowded street toward the camera. The camera holds in* M S *and reverse tracks as onlookers ask questions of the soldiers. Bawdy songs from nearby pleasure houses invade the sound track.*

O N L O O K E R 1 :   He looks like a great warrior. Whose clan does he belong to?

O N L O O K E R 2 :   Who is he?

R E T A I N E R (*holding Tobei's helmet*): The slayer of the renowned warrior Katsushige Fuwa. Tobei of Nakanosato, the most accomplished warrior in Lord Niwa's army. If you want good luck, give him your respect.

144.   C U :   *Tobei on horseback, basking in the adulation. The camera reverse tracks to* M L S *as Tobei, with a smug expression, leads his men past a brothel. An old woman, the proprietress, stops his horse.*

P R O P R I E T R E S S :   Pretty girls are waiting to entertain you. We have fine sake and fish. I won't let you pass. Many pretty women are waiting for you.

His retainers all crowd around Tobei.

R E T A I N E R 1 :   Chief—let us stay here.

T O B E I :   No! I'm going straight home. I want to show my success to my wife. I don't have time to spare.

R E T A I N E R 2 :   Chief, this is the time you should show your generosity.

R E T A I N E R 3 :   We all look forward to having a nice time!

T O B E I :   I see! Very well! I, Tobei Nakanosato, of the Niwa Camp, will rest here.

R E T A I N E R 2 :   Receive us with due respect.

Tobei dismounts and enters the brothel, followed by his men.

Inside the Brothel, evening

145.   M S :   *Tobei and his men in the background enter the main room of the brothel. The room is full of customers—samurai, foot soldiers, and townsmen—all singing and drinking sake, entertained by prostitutes. The camera pans left as Tobei and his cohorts walk left across the room and are seated, attended by women.*

146.   M S :   *another part of the brothel's main room. In the background, onlookers from the street poke their heads in through the open windows. They question the prostitutes gathered in the foreground.*

O N L O O K E R 1 :   Which one is Tobei?

O N L O O K E R 2 :   That one? What a brave exploit his was!

147. MCU: *the camera pans left and holds as several onlookers rush up to Tobei and bow to the floor. Tobei is drinking sake with a prostitute on his arm.*

ONLOOKER 1: May I have a sip from your cup for luck, sir?

ONLOOKER 2: May I, too?

ONLOOKER 3: I would like to, also.

Tobei extends his bowl.

ONLOOKER 1: Would you mind telling how you killed such a renowned warrior? We could use some pointers.

ONLOOKER 2: Please tell us, sir.

ONLOOKER 3: Please, sir.

TOBEI (*facing the camera*): Oh, there's not that much to say. First, you need a head—I mean brains! Then, it takes physical prowess. I mean—martial skills! (*He gestures dramatically.*) Then, there's speed. You have to know your chance and take it. (*Tobei stands, dominating the scene.*) A broad perspective on life can't hurt either. That way, you take it all in—in a glance. In sum, all you need is great brainwork! (*He pats his head.*) Understand?

ONLOOKER 1: Indeed, I've learned a valuable lesson.

TOBEI: There are many wise schools of strategy. Take the Kusunoki School of literature, for example. The Karama School of shooting, and

Otsubo School of strategy. Next, you need to know about fortification—
how to build castles, I mean!

*Tobei's speech merges with a song sung by a prostitute accompanied by a
samisen.*

Inside a Prostitute's Room, night

148. M L S : *a prostitute brushes her hair at frame left, while behind her back a
customer attempts to sneak away without paying for her services. She
grabs him, but he breaks free.*

P R O S T I T U T E : Don't run away.

C U S T O M E R : Let me go!

149. M C U : *outside the room we see the customer burst through the door, followed by the prostitute. The camera follows in* M S *as she pursues him into
the crowded main room. As the camera pans, it includes Tobei, who is
standing in the foreground, interrupted in the midst of his lecture.*

P R O S T I T U T E : I won't let you go. You had your fun, and now you want
to skip out without paying. You're lower than a common thief. Stop
him! Don't let him through!

*Other customers and prostitutes find this commotion entertaining. Tobei
moves in from frame left, watching closely.*

C U S T O M E R : I don't have money for a bitch like you!

He pushes the woman aside, but is stopped and made to return.

150. M C U *(low angle): The prostitute has managed to snag the customer's moneypouch. In the background, Tobei is seen watching in disbelief. As the customer is hustled away, the prostitute stands in the center of the frame counting her money.*

P R O S T I T U T E : Cheap bastard! But I've got my money now. Don't let me see you around here again!

She throws the empty pouch after him. Tobei, meanwhile, moves in closer. The woman suddenly turns toward him and they recognize each other. Stunned, Tobei realizes that she is his wife, Ohama.

T O B E I : Ohama!

Ohama turns away and stops, her back to the camera, and leans against a post. Tobei follows.

O H A M A : So, you look like a great man now, eh? So now you're the samurai you dreamed of. (*She turns to face Tobei. We see both of them in* M S *profile*). I had my own distinguished career while you were away fighting your way to the top. I wear pretty kimonos like this one. (*Again she steps away, turning her back to Tobei.*) I get to put on thick makeup, drink as much as I want, and sleep with a different man every night. How's that for achieving success as a woman?

Ohama turns and hurls her last words at Tobei. She runs out of the room, frame right. The camera tracks right as Tobei follows.

Back Entrance of the Brothel, night

151. M S : *Ohama stands outside the brothel, frame left. Tobei comes to her, center frame.*

O H A M A : I hope you're pleased with yourself! It must be wonderful seeing your dream come true. But of course fame costs something in suffering. And here I am, the great man's fallen wife. (*She grabs him by the arm.*) I know what! You can join the ranks of my customers tonight. Come on. Pay this fallen women some of the money you earned through your distinguished services!

She lets him go and falls to the ground, into M C U . *Tobei drops to his hands and knees next to her.*

T O B E I : Ohama! Listen! My success means nothing without you.

O H A M A (*looking at him*): Oh, sure. You only wanted to be a samurai. What a liar! You're never concerned about me!

The camera follows as she stands up and runs to a well where she attempts to throw herself in. Tobei grabs her and pulls her to the ground. He kneels over her in M L S .

T O B E I : No, honest. I thought you'd be proud of my success. I had no idea that you'd be reduced to this.

O H A M A : So now I'm defiled! (*She stands and moves toward the camera, into* M C U .) And you're to blame for it. So what can you do, restore my wifely purity? If you can't, then I'll just end it all.

Tobei comes to her side as she holds onto a tree for support.

TOBEI: Of course I can make amends. (*He holds her.*)

OHAMA (*sobbing and clutching the tree*): I wanted to kill myself so many times. But I couldn't, because I wanted to see you just one more time. I hated myself for that desire! (*She turns to face him, sobbing.*) Still I couldn't bear to kill myself without seeing you again! I couldn't die!

The music becomes louder, as she pushes against him and they fall to the ground in an embrace. The music ends.

Fade out.

A Shop in Omizo Castletown, day

Fade in.

152. MLS (*high angle*): *Genjuro is seated in the doorway of the kimono shop in the marketplace. People walk by in the street. He takes out his moneypouch as the shopkeeper displays his merchandise.*

153. MCU: *Genjuro and the shopkeeper are seated next to one another.*

SHOPKEEPER: Do you want all these?

GENJURO: I don't have quite that much on me. Can you knock a little off?

He offers some coins to the shopkeeper, who counts the money.

SHOPKEEPER: I can. I have to take this back.

The shopkeeper sets a box aside.

GENJURO: Oh, but I want that one, too. Come along with me to the Kutsuki mansion, and I'll pay you for it all.

SHOPKEEPER (*puzzled*): The Kutsuki mansion?

GENJURO: Yes, the house by the mountain.

The shopkeeper is visibly shocked. He replaces the box on top of the other purchases, then turns away from Genjuro.

SHOPKEEPER: Take it all, and just go! Take your money, too! Please, go away!

A Road Near the Town, evening

154. CU: *an old Buddhist priest walks away from the camera screen left into* MS *and passes Genjuro, who approaches the camera from the opposite direction. As they pass one another near a dilapidated gate, the priest glances at Genjuro, then turns and calls after him.*

PRIEST: Wait!

GENJURO (*looking back over his shoulder*): What do you want from me, Your Worship? (*He bows.*)

PRIEST (*approaching Genjuro*): I sense something terrible. You're headed for catastrophe.

GENJURO: What kind?

PRIEST: Let me take a closer look at your face.

GENJURO: My face?

PRIEST: Yes. I can't talk with you here. Come with me. (*He beckons to Genjuro.*)

GENJURO: Yes.

Genjuro follows the priest off frame left.

Dissolve.

A Temple, night

155. MCU: *the priest, sitting in the moonlight, facing the camera, talks to Genjuro whose back is to the camera. A Buddhist chant begins.*

PRIEST: What I see on your face is the shadow of approaching death. You haven't noticed anything unusual?

Genjuro raises his head and stares at the priest in bewilderment.

GENJURO: No, Your Worship!

PRIEST: Don't you have a home? Family? If so, rejoin them quickly. (*The priest stands and approaches Genjuro.*) If you stay here much longer, you'll die. Go quickly—home!

GENJURO: But why, Your Worship?

PRIEST: I just don't know. I only sense that you are about to lose your life!

GENJURO: But I am living happily with Lady Wakasa in the Kutsuki mansion.

PRIEST: But she is the ghost of someone dead.

Genjuro turns away. Courtly music merges with the chant.

GENJURO: I don't believe it!

The camera tracks as the priest circles around, kneels, and faces him. We see Genjuro's face in three-quarter profile, in the moonlight.

PRIEST: You have been beguiled by a forbidden kind of love. Don't you love your family? Do you want to sacrifice your wife and children and your life, too?

Genjuro gets up and starts to run away, but hesitates.

PRIEST: Wait! Go ahead if that's what you want so badly. But I can't watch you rush to such a terrible death. I'll exorcise the ghost. (*The priest turns Genjuro back.*) Come with me! If you see with your own eyes how horrible this dead spirit really is, you'll come to your senses.

The camera pans as the priest leads Genjuro into the temple and closes the door. The music stops.

Dissolve.

The Kutsuki Mansion, night

156. LS (*high angle*): *the camera looks down at the mansion and its courtyard. Lady Wakasa and Ukon glide along the lighted hallway. A chime begins, and continues until 158.*

157. MLS (*low angle*): *the camera pans right with Lady Wakasa as she enters a room to greet Genjuro and walks past the camera to a display of kimonos and other gifts. Ukon kneels in the background.*

LADY WAKASA (*fondling a kimono*): Ah! How lovely! (*She kneels next to Genjuro.*) Splendid crystals! I am so pleased!

UKON: You were so thoughtful! (*She takes a kimono and beckons to Lady Wakasa to try it on.*)

158. MCU: *with the kimono slipped over one shoulder, Lady Wakasa kneels by Genjuro. Her back is to the camera. We see his face.*

LADY WAKASA: I'm so relieved! I was afraid. You were so late getting home. (*Genjuro bows his head.*) You look worried. What has happened?

Genjuro is obviously disturbed. He begins to back away. Ukon comes out of the shadows, circles behind, and kneels next to him, her face in the light.

UKON: You had best not leave this place again. Since the downfall of our clan, we have been despised and slighted. We have even been cruelly slandered. People are so unkind!

159. MCU: *Lady Wakasa moves next to Genjuro.*

LADY WAKASA: Genjuro, I don't want to lose you! (*Pouts, then says decisively.*) Let's leave this house and go to my country place. (*Crossing behind Genjuro, she kneels to the left of him.*) There you will be my loving husband—forever! You will grant my wish, won't you, darling?

GENJURO: Forgive me! (*He turns away, rises, and starts to leave, but his path is blocked by Ukon. He stops, kneels, and bows to Lady Wakasa, who sits in the left foreground.*) Forgive me! I have deceived

you. I'm already married and have a child—back home. I left them behind in these war-torn times.

LADY WAKASA: Forget that now!

GENJURO: I implore you! Let me go home!

The chime stops.

160. MCU: *a reverse angle shot of Lady Wakasa. Harp music begins.*

LADY WAKASA: No. I forbid it. Come, dear. You will come with me to
my part of the country.

*She stands and approaches Genjuro as the camera reverse tracks, with
Ukon sitting in the background. She kneels beside him and puts her arm on
his back, but suddenly recoils in horror when she touches him. A chime
merges with the harp.*

LADY WAKASA: Ah!

UKON (*rushing to her*): My lady—what's the matter? (*The camera holds
in* MS.)

LADY WAKASA: There is something on his skin. Genjuro! You . . . you
have betrayed me!

*Ukon and Lady Wakasa close in on Genjuro, but he escapes to the next
room.*

161. MCU: *as Genjuro faces the camera, Ukon grabs him and tears away his
clothes. He falls to the floor. The camera holds in* MS. *Lady Wakasa
watches in the background.*

UKON: What's that on your skin? Remove it at once!

162. CU (*high angle*): *Genjuro lies on the floor. Sanskrit characters are painted
on his back.*

163. MS: *Ukon and Lady Wakasa stand over Genjuro, who lies on the floor in
the foreground.*

UKON: Why did you wed my ladyship when you had a wife already?

GENJURO: I don't know why I made such a terrible mistake.

UKON: A man's mistake is overlooked, but not a woman's . . .

GENJURO: Please forgive me! Let me go home!

Ukon kneels down.

UKON: No, we won't let you! Remove those Sanskrit characters. Or else
we'll never forgive you.

*Lady Wakasa sits down and leans over Genjuro, who lies trembling in a
fetal position. Ukon falls to the floor.*

LADY WAKASA: Genjuro, why have you betrayed me? You should be
my loving husband for ever and ever. Please . . .

UKON (*off*): Lady Wakasa left . . .

164. MCU (*low angle*): *Lady Wakasa kneeling over Genjuro.*

UKON (*off*): . . . this world before she knew what it was to be loved.

165. MCU: *Lady Wakasa's sad face reacts to Ukon's voice.*

UKON (*off*): I took pity on her. I wanted Her Ladyship to experience a woman's joy just once, even if briefly.

166. MCU: *as in 163. The camera pans left to Ukon, who leans over Genjuro, whose back is shown to the camera in the foreground.*

UKON: So I brought Her Ladyship back into this life. Finally, my wish for her came true when we found a fine man like you . . .

167. CU (*high angle*):   *Genjuro cowers on the floor. Sanskrit characters on his back face the camera.*

UKON (*off*):   . . . to be bound to her in eternal love. At long last her wish was fulfilled, and she has discovered the joy of being alive. If you leave her now, she will never be together with you.

168. MCU (*low angle*):   *Ukon continues her plea as Lady Wakasa watches, both leaning over Genjuro.*

UKON: Wouldn't your own heart break if you ruin Her Ladyship's new-found happiness? Think what terrible remorse you'll feel . . .

169. CU (*reverse angle*):   *Genjuro, from behind Lady Wakasa's shoulder, with his back strongly lighted.*

UKON (*off*):   Genjuro, I beg you. Dismiss such a treacherous thought, and stay with my lady forever . . .

170. MCU (*reverse angle*):   *as in 168. Genjuro scrambles away, frame left. Ukon and Lady Wakasa begin to chase him.*

GENJURO: Forgive me! Please forgive me!

171. MS: *in a panic, Genjuro tries to escape. We see him rush toward the camera. He reaches for a long sword on a stand, unsheathes it, turns, and slashes wildly in the direction of the women. He slices through a candle and the room goes dark.*

LADY WAKASA: Genjuro! (*Ignoring her entreaty, Genjuro pursues the woman, swinging his weapon blindly. Lady Wakasa cries out again.*) Genjuro! Genjuro!

172. MS: *still swinging wildly, Genjuro chases the women down a hallway. The camera shows Genjuro from behind: the women continue to back away from him.*

173. MS: *the camera tracks as Genjuro, still slashing with the sword, retreats from the house. He moves backwards, away from the camera, knocking over another candle and stumbling through a partition.*

174. MLS (*high angle*): *outside, from the courtyard, we see through the bare branches of a tree as Genjuro crashes through the partition. He falls off the porch and staggers away from the house, still brandishing his sword, only to faint and collapse on the ground. The music ends, accentuated with a gong.*

Ruins of the Kutsuki Mansion, morning

175. CU: *Genjuro's face. He has been asleep on the ground for some time. The camera pulls back to a high angle MS as Genjuro is awakened by a group of men: a Shinto priest, a local official, and his retainers. They take him into custody.*

OFFICIAL: You can't sleep here. Hey you—get up!

The men lift Genjuro to his feet. The Sanskrit marks are clearly visible on his body.

GENJURO: What are you doing?

PRIEST: You're a thief! You're under arrest for stealing that holy treasure from the shrine.

Genjuro attempts to break loose, but is surrounded. The camera holds in MLS. He points to the sword.

GENJURO: You're wrong. I didn't steal it.

PRIEST: Be quiet! This holy treasure has been missing for a month.

176. MCU (*low angle*): *in profile, Genjuro faces his accuser, who confronts him with the sword.*

GENJURO: You're mistaken. It belongs to Lady Wakasa of the Kutsuki clan. I didn't steal it.

PRIEST: The Kustuki clan? Are you lost in a dream? They were all destroyed. (*The priest turns and motions toward the ruins of the house.*) You're looking at the spot where the Kutsuki mansion stood.

Genjuro stares in disbelief.

OFFICIAL: Of course you're lying.

PRIEST (*lifting the sword*): Exactly where in that mansion did you find the treasure? He is a thief all right. Search him.

177. LS: *the men hold him. They take his leather moneypouch.*

GENJURO (*struggling*): Stop it! You're mistaken. That money is mine. Give it back!

OFFICIAL: We'd throw you into jail if the Shibata army hadn't burned it down.

PRIEST (*stepping forward*): You can be grateful for that much!

The camera pans with Genjuro as the men throw him to the ground by the ruins of the mansion.

178. MCU (*high angle*): *No music begins. Slowly, Genjuro stands, back to the camera, still showing the Sanskrit characters painted on his skin. He walks away from the camera as it tilts up into* LS, *surveying the scene. Only a few twisted, charred timbers of the burned-out mansion remain standing in a weedy field. On the sound track, we hear the song of Lady Wakasa.*

LADY WAKASA'S VOICE (*song*): The finest silk, of rarest shade, may fade away, . . . and quickly, too . . .

The camera pans to the right, following Genjuro as he roams the ruins. He finds remnants of the two kimonos he gave to Lady Wakasa. Astonished, he backs away, tripping over Lord Kutsuki's helmet, lying in the grass.

LADY WAKASA'S VOICE (*song*): . . . So may the love I offer you . . .

The camera cranes up into ELS *as Genjuro, shaken, stumbles away. Music ends.*

Fade out.

Genjuro's Village, night

Fade in.

179. LS: *Genjuro returning to his village. The camera pans left as he walks along the road. The village is quiet. He pauses by the kiln. It looks cold. He hurries on to his house. It looks dark and empty.*

180. MLS: *from inside the house we see Genjuro enter through the door. He calls for his wife.*

GENJURO: Miyagi! Miyagi!

The camera pans, first right, then left with Genjuro as he walks through the house, past the camera, and out the back door. In the same shot, the camera reverse pans right to the interior while we notice Genjuro through a window, circling around the outside of the house. As the camera returns in its pan to view the front door, we see light. Miyagi is cooking dinner at the hearth. Genjuro reenters the front door. Miyagi drops the chopsticks and runs to greet him. Music begins.

GENJURO: Forgive me. I have been away too long.

MIYAGI: Genjuro! Welcome home!

GENJURO: You must have been terribly worried!

MIYAGI: You made it back safely. I'm so glad.

GENJURO: Yes, I have made it home all right. (*He sits on the edge of the platform, near the hearth. Miyagi helps him remove his sandals.*) Where is Genichi?

MIYAGI: In bed!

GENJURO: Let me hold him.

Miyagi moves off screen right.

181. MLS: *the alcove where Genichi is sleeping. Miyagi picks him up and puts him in Genjuro's arms.*

MIYAGI: Your dad is back now!

GENJURO: Son—I'm back home!

They move to the hearth as Genjuro cradles the child. The camera tracks to hold them in MS. In the foreground, a kettle hangs over the fire. Miyagi reaches for a small bottle of sake behind the kettle.

GENJURO (*showing a small bundle*): I wanted so much to bring you both something much nicer. But this is all I could manage. I—I've made a great mistake.

MIYAGI: Don't say another word, my dear! You are back safe and sound. That's all that matters.

GENJURO (*weeping*): I've come to my senses. You were right. I have been so mixed up, so lacking in judgment.

MIYAGI: Please. No more. You must be tired. I've warmed some sake. (*Miyagi pours sake and Genjuro drinks.*) And I have some rice porridge ready. It's nice and warm.

The camera tracks in as she serves some food, then it pans very slowly to a MCU of Miyagi. She wipes tears from her eyes.

182. MS: *the three sit around the hearth, Miyagi with her back to the camera.*

GENJURO: What a relief! And sake never tasted so good. Ah, it's so quiet here. (*Genjuro is drifting off to sleep.*) Son—let me tuck you in. Since I left you, I've been all mixed up. Now I'm back home again! Back home! After so long!

He gets up. The camera pans left as he goes to a corner of the room to place Genichi in bed. Genjuro lies next to him, exhausted, and falls asleep. Miyagi crosses to place a blanket over them. The camera then pans right as she goes to the entryway near the hearth and places his straw sandals on the step. No music accentuated by a flute replaces the previous music. As the fire dies in the hearth, Miyagi sits in the darkness, alone. The straw sandals are seen in a spot of light in the foreground.

Dissolve.

183. MS: *in the darkness, Miyagi holds the kimono that Genjuro has taken off. She moves back to the center of the room, lights a candle, turns to look at her sleeping husband in the foreground, and starts mending the old robe.*

As the camera slowly cranes down, we see daylight dawning through the cracks in the walls.

184. LS: *the exterior of the house. It is morning.*
185. MLS: *from inside the house we see the village headman, with his servant, walk by the window. He pauses, looks in, and knocks on the door loudly.*

HEADMAN: Who's there? Open this door. Immediately!

Genjuro appears at frame right, barely awake. The fire has died in the hearth. He opens the door, and the headman and his servant enter.

GENJURO: Hello, sir!

HEADMAN: Genjuro! You're back!

GENJURO (*bowing*): Thank you for being so kind to my family while I was away.

The headman sees Genichi sleeping. Crossing in front of the camera, he goes to the child.

HEADMAN: Oh, here you are, son! I was really worried, wondering where you'd gone. I'm glad.

186. MS: *the headman kneels at the feet of the child. Genjuro kneels beside him.*

HEADMAN: I'm so glad. The boy must have sensed you came home.

Genjuro stands up and moves toward the camera into MCU as he calls for Miyagi. The headman comes toward him. Both are seen in profile.

HEADMAN: Are you dreaming, Genjuro?

GENJURO: What did you say, sir?

HEADMAN: You must know your wife was killed by a renegade soldier.

GENJURO (*shocked*): She was?

The headman bows his head and turns away. Genjuro crosses to the other side and faces him.

HEADMAN (*still looking at the ground*): If she were alive, she would be overjoyed to see you here again. Poor woman! May she rest in peace! (*Genjuro looks around, as if searching for Miyagi.*) Since Miyagi died, I have been taking care of your boy in my home. Suddenly last night he was gone. We were terribly worried. Something brought him here. How did he know that his father had returned?

The camera pulls back into MS as the headman kneels by the child and strokes his hair. Genjuro, stunned, goes to the hearth and waves his hand as if to touch something that is not there.

Fade out.

A Bridge, day

Fade in.

187. MS: *a suit of armor splashes down into a stream. The camera tilts up to reveal Tobei and Ohama standing on a bridge. Tobei angrily throws his weapons in the water. A Nō flute is heard.*

TOBEI: To hell with it!

OHAMA: You were too foolish to listen to me. Nothing I said made any difference. You had to learn from misfortune instead.

TOBEI: War made us ambitious in all the wrong ways!

They walk away from the bridge.

OHAMA: Please do profit from my sufferings. Be cheerful and work hard, won't you?

The camera pans right in LS *as they walk away along the riverbank. The drum, which now accompanies the No flute, beats louder.*

Fade out.

Miyagi's Grave, Day

Fade in.

188. MCU: *Genjuro is praying at Miyagi's grave. Incense is burning. He weeps.*

GENJURO: Miyagi, why did you die? Why?

A voice-over is heard on the sound track. It is Miyagi's voice.

MIYAGI'S VOICE: I'm not dead, my dear. I am with you. You are yourself once more. Just be the man you were, living and working where you belong. (*The camera slowly pulls back to show Genichi, also at the grave, in the left foreground.*) Hurry back to work!

Dissolve.

Genjuro's Workshop, day

189. MCU: *Genjuro is seen in profile throwing a pot on his wheel. Light comes through the window. In the background, in strong light, is a second wheel, motionless. Music starts.*

MIYAGI'S VOICE: What lovely shapes you make! My greatest delight is helping you at this wheel. How I yearn to see them fired! The firewood stands ready. No ruthless samurai threaten us now.

190. MCU: *the second potter's wheel sits motionless in the light.*

MIYAGI'S VOICE: So live in peace and make beautiful pottery.

Dissolve.

Outside Genjuro's Kiln, day

191. MS: *Genjuro is outside, feeding wood into the furnace of his kiln.*

MIYAGI'S VOICE: So much has happened to us. Now at last you have become the sort of the man I wanted you to be. But I am in another world now. That's how life works out, isn't it?

Genjuro inspects the fire. The camera pans right into LS *as he goes to his son, who is sitting nearby.*

Outside Genjuro's House, day

192. MS: *Tobei is working hard in the left foreground, tilling the soil. Ohama is cooking a meal in the background. She comes to Tobei.*

OHAMA: You must be exhausted. Rest for a bit.

TOBEI: Yes.

Ohama leaves frame right as the camera stays on Tobei.

193. MLS: *as Genjuro continues feeding his kiln, Ohama crosses in the foreground to frame right with a bowl of food for Genichi.*
    OHAMA: Here, my child. You'll like this. Eat while it's warm. (*She turns to Genjuro.*) You, too, brother, eat before it gets cold.
    Genichi picks up the bowl. The camera pans right, following as he runs to place it on his mother's grave nearby. He stops to pray and adjusts some flowers that are in a vase on the grave. As he does so, the camera slowly cranes up to reveal in ELS *the same pastoral scene that opened the film. Courtly music is still heard on the sound track.*
    End.

Contexts

Sources

Akinari Ueda (1734–1809), a scholar and a man of letters in eighteenth-century Japan, is best known for *Tales of Moonlight and Rain (Ugetsu Monogatari,* 1776). Consisting of nine ghost stories, this work was highly influenced by Chinese colloquial fiction and Japanese Buddhist tales in subject matter, rhetoric, and structure. However, to these literary elements derived from two different traditions, Ueda successfully adds his own keen sense of the supernatural. It is this amalgamation that makes *Tales of Moonlight and Rain* a work of artistic excellence in the genre known as *yomihon,* a narrative form that emerged between the late eighteenth century and the early nineteenth century as a forerunner of modern popular romance.

Included in this volume are two stories from Ueda's collection—"The House Amid the Thickets" (Asaji ga Yado) and "The Lust of the White Serpent" (Jasei no In)—which served as literary sources for Mizoguchi's *Ugetsu.* "The Lust of the White Serpent" alone has been adapted by other filmmakers three times, the earliest version being Thomas Kurihara's work (1921) of the same title.

The House Amid the Thickets

In the province of Shimōsa, district of Katsushika, village of Mama, during the Kyōtoku Era, there once lived a man named Katsushirō. Ever since his grandfather's time the family had dwelled here in prosperity, owning many fields and much rice land. But the youthful Katsushirō was lazy; he disliked working the land and regarded such labour as a dreary task. In consequence, his wealth declined; his relations had less and less to do with him. Eventually he grew ashamed of himself and longed to find some means or other by which he might restore his family's fortunes.

Around this time, a man named Sasabe no Sōji, who travelled each year from the capital to buy Ashikaga dyed silk, happened to make one of his frequent visits to the village of Mama, where his kinsfolk lived. Having met him on previous occasions, Katsushirō asked Sasabe to take him to Kyoto as a merchant. Sasabe agreed quite readily and said, 'We can leave whenever you're ready.'

Because he knew that Sasabe was a reliable man, Katsushirō was pleased at his reply. He soon sold his remaining rice fields, spent the money on bolts of white silk, and prepared to depart for Kyoto. His wife, Miyagi, who was beautiful enough to stop any man's eyes, had always taken good care of Katsushirō, but at this decisive moment she disapproved of his purchase of goods and of his projected journey to Kyoto. She did her best to dissuade him, but in the face of his impetuous nature all her efforts were in vain, and so, though deeply distressed by the uncertainty of her own future, she faithfully helped him to get ready.

'While you're gone I shall have no one to turn to,' said Miyagi on their last night before the painful parting. 'My heart is sure to wander long among the moors and mountains, and it will be a lonesome time for me. Remember me day and night and hurry back. I shall pray with all my heart for your good health; no one knows what tomorrow may bring. Be resolute, but still, feel pity for me.'

'You know how I shall drift, as if on floating wood, and stay long in unknown provinces,' Katsushirō replied, consoling her, 'but when the leaves begin to turn, in the fall, I'll come back. Please have courage while you wait,' and as dawn broke in the cock-crowing land of Azuma, he left and hurried toward the capital.

In the summer of that year fighting broke out in Kamakura between the Lord Shigeuji and Governor Uesugi. After his mansion had been burned to the ground, Shigeuji was forced to withdraw to Shimōsa, where he had strong support, and the entire East was suddenly thrown into turmoil. Young men were conscripted as

From *Ugetsu Monogatari* by Akinari Ueda, trans. Leon Zolbrod (Tuttle: Tokyo & Rutland, 1974), pp. 121–132. Copyright © by George Allen and Unwin.

soldiers, and more and more it became a matter of every person for himself; old people fled to take refuge in the hills, and the word would spread, 'Today the army will burn our village,' or, 'Tomorrow enemy troops are coming,' and women and children ran here and there, crying in consternation and anguish.

Miyagi wondered if she too shouldn't take safety somewhere, but she trusted in her husband's bidding to wait until autumn, and though her heart was filled with anxiety, she remained at home, counting each day. But after the autumn winds came and Miyagi still heard no tidings, she lamented in disappointment, 'He too has grown as fickle as the inconstant world,' and she wrote,

Mi no usa wa	I cannot convey
hito shimo tsugeji	The bitterness of my sorrow,
Ōsaka no	But would you point out to him—
yū zuke tori yo—	Songbird of evening—
aki mo kurenu to	That autumn is almost over.

Still, many provinces separated Miyagi from her husband, and there was no one with whom she could send word.

After the outbreak of war people's ways changed for the worse. A man who from time to time had visited the house and knew of Miyagi's beauty tried to seduce her, but she staunchly kept her moral standards and succeeded in remaining faithful. From then on, she bolted her door and refused to see any visitors.

Meanwhile, her maidservant had left. She used up her small hoard of savings, and though the old year ended, things were still unsettled in the new one. During the previous autumn, Shogun Yoshimasa had ordered Tō no Tsuneyori, Lord of Shimotsuke, who held Gujō, in the province of Mino, to take the imperial banner and go to his domains in Shimotsuke. From here, he made preparations with his clansman, Chiba no Sanetane, to attack Shigeuji, but the latter put up a staunch defence, and no one knew when the war might end. Bands of outlaws everywhere pillaged and burned settlements and built fortifications. No place in the Eight Provinces remained safe, and throughout the wretched world there was great destruction.

Having arrived in Kyoto with Sasabe, Katsushirō soon sold all of his silk, because around this time in the capital there was a great demand for luxuries. He made a good profit and was preparing to return East, when he heard reports that Uesugi's troops had taken the Kamakura Palace and pursued Shigeuji to an area around his home, which had become the centre of a raging battle. 'It's like the crossroads of Cho Lu,' people said. Katsushirō knew that even rumours about local events were often exaggerated, and that there was no telling what had happened in a place as far away as the distant white clouds; but he nevertheless felt uneasy when he left the capital at the beginning of the Eighth Month.

On the all-day climb over lovely Kiso hill, a band of robbers barred his way and stripped him of everything he possessed. In addition, he heard that further east new barriers had been set up here and there and that travellers were forbidden to pass. Now he had no means of sending word to his wife. 'Perhaps,' he thought, 'my home has been lost in the fires of war, and Miyagi is no longer living in this world, and my native village now serves as a dwelling place for demons.' Thereupon, once again he turned toward Kyoto, but when he reached Musa, in the province of Ōmi, he suddenly fell ill, stricken with the fever.

In that village there lived a wealthy man named Kodama Yoshibei, who was Sasabe's father-in-law, and Katsushirō implored his help. Kodama took him in, summoned a physician, and paid for all the medicines. When Katsushirō's fever had at last subsided, he thanked his benefactor profusely; but he was still not well enough to travel, and he had no choice but to stay there until spring. Meantime, because people liked his straightforward nature and his amiable disposition, he began to make friends in the village, and not only Kodama but others as well valued his company. Later he went to Kyoto and called on Sasabe; afterward he returned to Ōmi and took lodging with Kodama, and before he knew it seven years had gone by as if in a dream.

It was now the second year of Kanshō. The Hatakeyama brothers, in the province of Kawachi, near the capital, were engaged in a dispute, and trouble threatened the area around Kyoto. Also, in the spring of the same year plague spread out of control, and corpses lay piled in the streets. People believed that the end of the world was coming, and they grieved at the transience of life. Katsushirō thought, 'How degenerate I've grown! What use have I made of my life? I've done nothing, and here I am in a distant province living off the charity of a stranger. How long can I go on this way? I don't know what has become of my wife, who I left in my native village, and by staying these long years in fields that grow the grass of forgotten love, how can I think of myself as a reliable person! Even though Miyagi may be dead and everything changed, I must at least go and find out and make her a grave mound.'

Katsushirō told his friends about his decision, and during a spell of fine weather in the Rainy Month, he took his leave, reaching his native place in little more than ten days. He neared his former home late one day when the sun had already set in the west and rain clouds hung low, almost touching the earth, making the evening unusually dark. But this was, after all, his old familiar village, and as he crossed the summer moorland it scarcely occurred to him that he might lose his way. A bridge that once spanned the rapid stream had now collapsed; to be sure, no sound of horses' hooves could be heard. The fields lay desolate and abandoned, and he could barely tell which way the path led. Although most of the dwellings were gone, in several of those that still stood here and there he noticed some sign of life. Virtually nothing, however, looked at all familiar, and after standing and wondering which house might be his, he retraced his steps about twenty paces. There, by the starlight that shone through a rift in the clouds, he at last recognised the tall pine tree that had been split by lightning—the landmark of his home. Joyfully, he went toward the house and saw that it had not changed, and he could tell that someone was inside, because through the chinks in the old door he spied gleams of light from a flickering lantern. 'What if it's a stranger? Can it possibly be her?' he thought, trembling with anticipation. He approached the door, clearing his throat as he did so, and from inside immediately came a voice saying, 'Who is there?'

True, it sounded aged and decrepit, but he knew unmistakably that it belonged to Miyagi. 'Can I be dreaming?' he wondered, his heart in turmoil, and he shouted, 'I've come back! It's a miracle that you've survived, unchanged, living alone in this wilderness.' Miyagi recognised his voice and without delay opened the door. She looked black and dirty, with sunken eyes and hair that hung dishevelled down her back. He wondered if she were, indeed, the same person. When she saw Katsushirō, Miyagi without saying a word uncontrollably began to weep.

Astonished, Katsushirō, too, was silent for a long time, and at last he whispered, 'Had I thought that you were still alive, I wouldn't have waited so many years. When I was in Kyoto I heard about the fighting at Kamakura, and how when Shigeuji was defeated he fell back to Shimōsa and that Uesugi kept pressing the attack. At the beginning of the Eighth Month I took leave of Sasabe and set out from Kyoto, but on the Kiso Highway robbers took all my money and clothing, and I barely escaped with my life. Then I learned from villagers that along the Eastern Sea Road and the Eastern Mountain Road new barriers had been set up and travellers were being turned back. I also found out that Tō no Tsuneyori had been sent to help Uesugi fight against Shigeuji. I heard that our province was nothing but scorched earth, and that horses had trampled every foot of ground. You must have passed away to dust and ashes, I thought, or if not that, I imagined, perhaps you had drowned. Eventually I went back to Kyoto where I managed to live for seven years on other people's good will. But recently I found myself wondering more and more about old times, and I decided that the least I could do was to return and pay my respects. Even in my wildest dreams, you see, I never imagined that you might still be alive. Surely, you must be like the cloud of Witches Hill or the apparition at the Palace of Han?' Thus did he try to explain his behaviour.

'Soon after you left,' said Miyagi, holding back her tears, 'before the autumn I begged you to return by, trouble broke loose in the world. The villagers fled from their homes to take to the seas or to find refuge in the mountains, and the few men who stayed mostly behaved like brutes. No doubt feeling bold because I was now living alone, someone tried to trick me with flattering words, but I knew that I would rather die as a broken jewel than go on living as common clay. Many times I had to bear heartache and sorrow. When the Milky Way told of autumn, you had not returned, so I waited through winter. But spring came and there was still no news. I thought of going to Kyoto to find you, but even a strong man could not loosen the barrier locks, and there was no way at all for a woman to get past. I stayed here, like the pine outside the house, waiting with the owls and foxes, until today in vain. But now that you've come back, I'm delighted, and all my reproaches for you are forgotten. I'm very happy now, but you should know that a woman could die of yearning, and a man can never know her agony.'

Again she broke into weeping, and Katsushirō took her in his arms and comforted her, saying, 'These nights are the shortest of all,' and they lay down together. In the cool darkness the window paper rustled as the breeze whispered through the pines. Exhausted from his travel, Katsushirō fell into a sound sleep. Around the fifth watch, however, when the sky began to grow light, he suddenly became partially aware of the world of the senses. He vaguely knew that he was cold, and groping with his hands, he tried to pull up the covers. But to his surprise leaves rustled beneath his touch, and as he opened his eyes a cold drop of something fell on his face.

He wondered if it were rain coming in, and then he noticed that the roof was gone, as though torn away by the wind, and that it was daybreak, and the pale shining moon of dawn still remained in the sky. All of the shutters to the house were gone, and through spaces in the dilapidated latticework bed there grew high grass and weeds. The morning dew had fallen and soaked his sleeves wringing wet. The walls were covered with ivy and vines, and the garden was buried in tall madder weed. The season was still late summer, but the desolation of the house reminded him of autumn moors.

'Miyagi is not here! Where could she have gone?' he thought, upon finding that she no longer lay with him. 'Have I been bewitched by a fox?'

Although it had been long deserted, the dwelling was without a doubt his old home. He recognised its spacious interior, its walls, and even the storehouse—all of which he had built to suit his own particular tastes. Bewildered and uncertain and scarcely knowing where he stood, he slowly realised that Miyagi was surely dead and that this was now the home of foxes and badgers—and perhaps, too, of fearsome evil spirits who had entered this desolate place and taken the form of his wife. 'Or was it her ghost,' he thought, 'her ghost yearning for love that came back to meet me. It was just as I remembered her,' and in an excess of grief, he began to weep.

'It is only I, I alone who remain unchanged,' he muttered, as he searched—first here, then there. Finally, in what had been the sleeping quarters he saw her grave, a heaped up mound of earth, which someone had covered by boards removed from the verandah in order to give protection from rain and dew. 'Is this where her ghost came from last night?' he wondered, horrified and yet entranced.

Amid the implements that had been placed there to dispense holy water, he found a crude strip of wood with a slip of old and tattered Nasumo paper. Although patches of the writing had faded away and some of the characters were hard to read, he recognised his wife's hand. No holy name and no date were there, but merely thirty-one syllables that showed sharp awareness of approaching death:

Sari-tomo to	I have wept in sorrow,
omou kokoro ni	Longing for him to come back,
hakararete	But how can I go on living
yo ni mo kyō made	In this world, till now deceived
ikeru inochi ka	By vain hopes of his return!

Recognising for the first that Miyagi was in fact dead, he flung himself to the ground, weeping bitterly and lamenting how cruel it was not even to have knowledge of the day or the year on which she had perished. At last he stopped weeping, and arose. The sun had climbed high in the sky, and walking to the nearest house, he saw the man who lived there and realised that it was not one of the old residents, but he wondered if he perhaps knew.

'Where are you from?' demanded the other man, before Katsushirō had a chance so speak.

'I used to be the master of the house next door,' Katsushirō replied with a bow, 'but I've spent the past seven years in Kyoto on business and just came back last night, only to find that my place is in ruins and no one lives there. It seems that my wife has died and that someone made a grave, but I wish that I knew just when it all happened. If you by chance have heard, I wonder if you'd please tell me?'

'You must feel terribly upset,' the man said, 'but I haven't lived here for even a year, and I suppose that her death must have taken place quite a while before I came. I don't know much at all about the previous residents, for almost everyone who used to inhabit this village fled when the fighting broke out, and a great majority of the people who now make their home here came from elsewhere. Still, there's an old man who seems to have stayed. Sometimes he goes to your house and prays for the salvation of a departed soul. Perhaps he can tell you about your wife.'

'Then, could you please show me where this old man lives?' Katsushirō asked.

'About a hundred paces toward the seashore there are many hemp fields that he has planted,' the man explained, 'and nearby you'll find a small hut where he dwells.'

Feeling a sense of relief, Katsushirō made his way there and discovered an old man of about seventy years of age whose back was piteously bent seated on a round woven mat, sipping tea in front of his open-air fireplace. As soon as he recognised Katsushirō, he asked, 'Why did you take so long to come back?'

Katsushirō then saw that this was Grandfather Uruma, who had long resided in the village, and he greeted the old man politely and described how he had gone to Kyoto and stayed, quite contrary to his original intentions. Katsushirō told him of his strange experience the night before and began to thank him for having said prayers, but he could no longer hold back his tears.

'Soon after you went far away,' Grandfather Uruma explained, 'in the summer, I think it was, raging battle broke out, and the villagers scattered and fled. All of the young men were conscripted, and the mulberry fields quickly changed back into thickets fit for foxes and rabbits. But your brave wife trusted that you would keep your promise to return by fall and refused to desert her home. Because my legs are lame and I have trouble walking even a hundred steps, I too shut myself up tightly and never left. Although tree spirits and other fearsome monsters at one time established themselves in your place, that young woman continued to stay on, though I never in my whole life saw anything more pitiable. Autumn passed;

then spring came, and that year on the Tenth Day of the Eighth Month she died. Grieving desperately at her loss, I carried soil with my own decrepit hands and buried her in a coffin. To mark the grave mound I used a verse that she herself had composed before she passed away. I did my best to assemble some things for prayer and for dispensing holy water, but because I never learned how to write even a little, I had no way of recording the date, and the nearest temple is so far away that I could not get a name for her memory. Five years have since passed, but judging from what you've said, no doubt your brave wife's ghost has visited you to tell you of the anguish that she suffered. Let us go back once again and pray with all our heart.'

So saying, the old man took up his staff and led the way. The pair of them knelt in front of the grave, lifting up their voices in lament and chanting prayers all night, until the dawn. As they kept their vigil in the darkness, the old man told Katsushirō a story:

'Long before even my grandfather's grandfather was born, bygone ages ago, there lived in this village a beautiful maiden named Mama no Tegona. Her family was poor, and she wore dresses made of hemp, and collars fixed with blue. Although her hair went uncombed and she walked unshod, her face was as perfect as the moon when at the full, and her smile was like the fragrance of the flowers. Because she surpassed even the ladies of the capital, clad in their rich brocades, she was courted not only by the men of this village but also by guardsmen from the capital and even by men from neighbouring provinces, who conveyed their love and longed for her. But Tegona grew sad and despondent that she could not give her heart to the suitor of her choice, and she cast herself into the waves in the bay. Struck by the way that her fate reflected the sorrow of life, many poets of old wrote verses about her, and the legend has been handed down. When I was a boy and my mother told it to me, I used to listen, enthralled, and filled with pity for the young woman. Yet now I feel that your wife Miyagi's fate was sadder by far even than that of innocent young Tegona of old.'

While speaking, Grandfather Uruma wept profusely, unable to stop, losing control of his emotions as old people so easily do. Katsushirō, upon hearing the story, was also beside himself with grief, and in the clumsy style of a man from the provinces, he made a poem:

Inishie no	No matter how much
Mama no Tegona wo	They loved Tegona
kaku bakari	In that bygone age,
koite shi aran	I loved my dear wife
Mama no Tegona wo	Every bit as much.

Of his true feelings he could scarcely express a small part, but in some ways his plaintive cry may have been more genuine than poems by far more skilful hands.

The story of Miyagi and Katsushirō was brought back by merchants who from time to time have paid visits to that province.

The Lust of the White Serpent

Once upon a time, though it matters not exactly when, in the province of Kii, by the cape of Miwa, there lived a fisherman named Ōya no Takesuke. He was rich in the luck of the sea and took care of many other fishermen who caught all sorts of things, broad of fin and narrow of fin, thus enabling his house to prosper. Takesuke had two sons and one daughter. His first son, Tarō, was a simple but hard-working man, and his second child, a girl, had married someone from the province of Yamato, where she now lived. The third child, named Toyoo, grew to be a gentle young lad, especially fond of polite accomplishments but with little practical sense.

'If I gave him his share of the inheritance,' the father lamented, 'it would soon pass into other hands. Even should another family adopt him to continue their line, I would eventually grow ill from hearing uncomplimentary reports. The best thing to do would be to let him develop in his own way and become a scholar or a priest, if he pleases, and for the rest of his life Tarō could look after his needs.' From then on he made no effort to restrain his son.

Toyoo had a teacher who was a priest at the Shingū Shrine. His name was Abe no Yumimaro, and Toyoo visited him regularly. On one of these trips, around the end of the Ninth Month, when the sea was especially calm, clouds suddenly arose from the southeast, and a light drizzle began to fall. Therefore, as he set out from his master's home Toyoo borrowed a large umbrella, but by the time he came in sight of the Asuka Shrine, the rain had grown so heavy that he decided to seek shelter at a nearby fisherman's hut.

'Oh, it's the master's younger son,' said the old man who came to the door. 'Your visit is indeed an honour for such a humble place as mine. Please come in and sit down.' He took out a shabby round cushion from which he shook the dust and offered it to Toyoo.

'The rain will surely stop soon, and I'll be all right, so please don't put yourself out for me,' Toyoo protested as he accepted the old man's hospitality.

Then, strange to relate, a sweet voice came from outside saying, 'Please give me some shelter for a little while,' and a young lady entered. She seemed to be not yet in her twentieth year. She was very beautiful and she had lovely long hair and was dressed in an elegant kimono printed with a pattern representing distant mountains. A pretty maid fourteen or fifteen years old carrying a bundle wrapped in cloth accompanied her, and the pair looked drenched and bedraggled. When the

From *Ugetsu Monogatari* by Akinari Ueda, trans. Leon Zolbrod (Tuttle: Tokyo & Rutland, 1974), pp. 160–184. Copyright © by George Allen and Unwin.

young woman saw Toyoo, her face flushed with embarrassment, betraying her fine breeding.

Toyoo felt an impulsive stir of excitement, and he thought to himself, 'I've never heard of such a splendid lady living nearby. I suppose she has come from the capital on a journey to the Three Holy Places and has decided to visit this area in order to enjoy the seaside. But it's certainly unusual that she has no man to accompany her.' He said, 'By all means, make yourself comfortable,' stepping back as he spoke. 'The rain should stop soon.'

'I hope you won't mind the intrusion,' said the young lady, and it being a small hut, the pair sat facing one another. The more Toyoo gazed on her, the more he was struck by her ethereal beauty.

'You appear to be of noble birth,' said Toyoo, utterly bewitched. 'Are you on a pilgrimage to the Three Holy Places, or on your way to the Minenoyu Hot Springs? What can you find to admire by a barren coast such as this? After all, a poet of bygone days wrote:

Kurushikumo	How painful it is,
furi kuru ame ka	This rain that pelts on me
Miwa ga saki	At Miwa's rugged cape,
Sano no watari ni	And by the Sano Crossing
ie mo aranaku ni	No cottage appears in sight.

That day must have been as dreary as this one. Even though this is a lowly hut, the master is indebted to my father, so rest yourself until the rain is over. Meantime, do you mind if I ask where you plan to stay tonight? It might appear improper for me to escort you, but you may certainly borrow my umbrella.'

'How generous of you,' the young lady replied. 'Your thoughtfulness makes me feel as if I were already dry. I'm not from the capital, however. I have lived nearby for quite a while, and thinking that it was a splendid day, I went to Nachi to pray. On my way home in my fright at this sudden shower I had no idea where I might seek shelter, and I inexplicably found myself here. My home isn't far away, and now that the downpour has let up somewhat, I must be going.'

'Do take the umbrella,' Toyoo urged, 'since the rain hasn't completely stopped. I'll get it sometime later. Please tell me where you live, and I may send someone for it.'

'Around Shingū just ask anyone for Agata no Manago's house,' replied the young lady. 'It's growing dark, and I shall take advantage of your kindness and use this on my way.' Accepting the umbrella, she departed as Toyoo watched anxiously. He then borrowed a straw raincoat from his host and returned home.

Toyoo found himself unable to forget even the slightest detail of Manago's appearance. After a fitful night's sleep, toward dawn he dreamed of visiting her house. The entrance and the dwelling itself looked large and grand, with the shutters tightly drawn and the screens lowered, as though she lived in comfort and elegance. Manago emerged to greet him, saying, 'I couldn't forget your kindness, and I was hoping that you might come. Please enter.' and leading him inside, she served him wine and various fruits until he felt pleasantly intoxicated. She furnished him a pillow, and they lay down together. When Toyoo awoke from his dream, he found that it was morning.

'If only it were true!' he thought, and completely forgetting about breakfast, he went out, disturbed and agitated, and he walked to the village of Shingū, where he repeatedly inquired for Agata no Manago's palace. No one, however, knew where it was, and afternoon came while he was still searching laboriously. Then he noticed Manago's young maidservant walking toward him from the east.

'Where does your mistress live?' Toyoo asked, rejoicing to see her. 'I thought that I'd come by for the umbrella.'

'How kind of you,' replied the maid, with a smile. 'Please follow this way,' and presently she led him to an imposing gate in front of a spacious dwelling and said to him, 'here is where we live.' The building corresponded in every detail, down to the tightened shutters and the lowered screens, to the palace he had seen in his dream, and he marvelled at this as he entered.

'The gentleman who lent us the umbrella has called, and I have brought him here,' the maid announced, hurrying inside.

'Where is he? Show him in,' said Manago, as she appeared.

'I'm sorry to bother you,' said Toyoo, 'but I was on my way to visit Master Abe, who has been my teacher for several years, and thinking that I might pick up the umbrella and return it to him, I decided to stop by. Now that I know where you live, I'll call again sometime.' and he seemed determined to withdraw.

Manago, however, demanded that he remain and said, 'Maroya, don't let him go.'

'Didn't you urge us to take the umbrella?' said the maid, blocking Toyoo's way. 'Now in exchange we insist that you stay here,' and she took him to the southern front room, where floor mats had been arranged. The curtains, the articles in the cabinet, and the design on the drapery were all of the best quality and classical fashion and marked the owner of the house as no commoner.

'It so happens that my husband has died,' said Manago, reappearing, 'and therefore I can't entertain you with a proper feast, but at least let me offer you a cup of poor wine.'

Tall dishes and flat dishes of exquisite taste, each filled with delicacies from the sea and the mountains, and ceramic cups with a jar of wine were all set before him, after which Maroya began to serve the food and drink. Toyoo was beside himself with wonder and could hardly believe all that was taking place. Guest and host alike became flushed with wine, and as Manago raised her cup to Toyoo, her features looked as lovely as a garland of cherry blossoms reflected in the water; a smile rippled on her lips like a spring breeze, and her voice sounded as sweet as a nightingale soaring and flitting among the trees.

'Although it embarrasses me very much, there is something that I must tell you,' she proceeded to say. 'After all, if I were not truthful and consequently fell ill, what innocent god might have to endure unjust accusations? Even though I frankly reveal my feelings towards you, you mustn't take me to be inconstant in my affections—on the contrary. I lost both of my parents while still an infant in the capital. I was brought up by my nurse and married to a man named Agata, a subordinate to the governor of this province. Three years have already passed since I came here with him, and this spring before his term of office expired he died after a brief illness, leaving me to fend for myself. I have heard that in the meantime my nurse became a nun and left the capital to practice her austerities elsewhere, so you can understand that even my native place is no longer home to me. But because you were so kind in sheltering me from the rain yesterday, I know that you are a generous man, and I want to devote the rest of my life to serving you. If you'll take me even though I was married before, I want to pledge a thousand years of love with you.'

Already excited with the idea of Manago's becoming his wife, Toyoo felt his heart stir as if a bird rising from its nest. But he was not free to do as he wished; he needed his father and his brother's permission to marry. His happiness immediately gave way to sorrow, and he said nothing to Manago.

Obviously upset, Manago hurriedly added, 'I'm ashamed that I can't take back what I said. I shouldn't have shown what foolish ideas I have in my poor heart. It was a terrible mistake of me to cause you so much distress, and I wish that I could call on the sea to rise and cover me. Although I meant everything I said, think of it as the result of the wine's heat. Let us forget about the whole matter.'

'I thought from the start,' Toyoo replied, 'that you came from a good family in the capital, and now I see that I was right. It's unbelievable that someone raised as I was along the lonely seashore visited mainly by whales should ever receive such an attractive proposal. But I couldn't answer you directly, because I'm dependent on my father and elder brother, and except for my skin and bones there is nothing that I can call my own. I have no prospects or resources to support you with, and I possess no special talent—all of which causes me great regret. But if you are willing to accept someone like me and suffer come what may, I shall love and cherish you forever. When one stumbles on the hill of love, as did even Confucius, he forgets about both filial piety and his very life itself.'

'I'm delighted that you should make such a promise,' she said. 'In spite of my inadequacies, please come often and stay with me. Meantime, here is something that my former husband prized as a matchless treasure. Keep it with you, always,' and she gave him a precious antique sword ornamented with gold and silver. Feeling that it would be unlucky to refuse such a gift at the beginning, Toyoo accepted the object.

'Tonight you must stay here with me,' Manago implored, but Toyoo replied,

'My father would punish me if I spent the night away without his permission. Tomorrow evening I'll find some pretext for coming,' and he took his leave. Toyoo again found himself unable to fall asleep before dawn.

Early in the morning when Tarō arose to oversee the fishermen and passed by the partly open door to Toyoo's bedroom, he happened to glance inside. By the glow of the fading lamplight he caught a glimpse of the sword, which Toyoo had placed next to his pillow while he slept. 'How strange,' thought Tarō, with considerable apprehension, 'where did he ever get such a thing?' At the sound of his noisily opening the door all the way, Toyoo awoke.

'Did you call me?' he asked, seeing his brother.

'Why do you have that sword by your pillow?' Tarō said. 'It's improper to keep such an extravagant thing in a fisherman's house. If father finds out, you know what he'll say.'

'But I wasted so money on it. I didn't buy it,' protested Toyoo. 'Someone gave it to me yesterday, and I merely brought it home.'

'How would anyone around here ever present you a treasure like this?' replied Tarō. 'In the past you've even wasted money on bothersome Chinese books, but because father rarely says anything to you, up till now I haven't complained either. If you expect to wear this sword on parade in the great shrine festival, you must be out of your mind!' he shouted, raising his voice so loudly that their father heard.

'What has the wastrel done this time?' said the father. 'Tarō, send him in to me.'

'I don't know where on earth he got it,' Tarō replied, 'but Toyoo bought a shiny sword, such as a general might have, and that's no good. You should ask him about it and get to the bottom of things. I'll go and see that the fishermen aren't idle,' and so saying, he departed.

Then the mother called Toyoo and said, 'Why did you buy such a thing? All of our rice and money belongs to Tarō. What do you have that you can call your own? Every day we allow you to do as you wish, but if you continue to make Tarō angry, where under the sun could you ever find a place to live? As someone who has had the benefit of education, why can't you understand that much?'

'But really, mother, I didn't buy it,' Toyoo said. 'A certain person gave it to me, for a reason, and when Tarō saw it, he falsely accused me.'

'What did you do, then,' the father shouted, 'that someone should give you such a treasure? That makes the matter even worse. You'd better tell me all about it immediately.'

'But to explain it just now would be very embarrassing. I'd rather speak to someone else.'

'To whom can you tell anything that you won't say to your elder brother or to me?' said the father, with irritation.

At this point, Tarō's wife, who was also present, restored the calm by taking Toyoo aside, reassuring him, 'Although I may not be able to help, come and explain things to me.'

'Even before Tarō found the sword and raised a fuss,' said Toyoo to his sister-in-law, 'I had wanted to talk to you privately and tell you about what happened, but meantime I'm already in trouble. Actually, I got the blade from a young lady who is living alone and has asked me if I would look after her. But I'm completely at a loss, because I have no experience, and if I became involved without permission, I'd be mercilessly disowned. Please try to understand.'

His sister-in-law smiled at him and said, 'I've always thought it a pity that you aren't married, and I'm happy for your sake. Although it may be beyond my power, I'll try to convey your feelings to the others.'

That night when she explained the situation to Tarō she said, 'Don't you agree that this is good news? I hope that you'll do your best to convince father.'

'I don't like the idea,' replied Tarō, obviously upset. 'I've never heard of anyone by the name of Agata in the service of the governor of this province, and we should certainly have learned of such a person's death, considering that father is the headman of the village. But first of all, go and bring me the sword.' She immediately carried it in, and after examining it carefully, Tarō sighed and said in a worried voice, 'This is terrible. Recently, a great minister in the capital offered prayers and donated many valuable objects to our shrine, but it seems that these sacred treasures have suddenly disappeared from the storehouse, and the head priest has reported the theft to the governor of the province. In order to find the thief the governor has commanded his deputy, Bunya no Hiroyuki, to go to the head priest's mansion, and I know that they've been working hard on the case. This sword is certainly not the sort of object a petty official would use. We must show it to father.' Taking the weapon to his father, he explained matters and said, 'In such a horrifying predicament, have you anything to suggest?'

'What a dreadful thing to happen!' said the father, his face turning pale. 'Up till now Toyoo has never stolen so much as a single hair. Through what sin of ours should he turn to such evil? But if anyone else reports him, it will mean the end of our entire house. For the sake of our ancestors and descendants, we can't be sentimental over an unfilial son. Turn him in tomorrow.'

First thing in the morning. Tarō went to the head priest's mansion to tell what had happened and present the sword for examination. The head priest said in amazement, 'Yes, this is the same blade that the nobleman gave to us.'

'We must question him about the other lost goods,' said the governor's deputy when he was informed, 'so arrest the suspect,' and dispatching ten warriors, he had Tarō show them the way. Meanwhile, unaware of these events, Toyoo was reading when the warriors burst in to take him away.

'What have I done?' he protested, though in vain, as they placed him in bonds, while the father, the mother, Tarō, and the sister-in-law stood by in confusion and sorrow over such misfortune.

'The court has summoned you,' said one of the warriors. 'Hurry up, move,' and forming a cordon around the prisoner, they escorted him to the head priest's mansion, where the deputy glared at Toyoo.

'By stealing a sacred treasure,' he said, 'you have committed a terrible crime. Now confess in full where you have hidden the remainder of your loot.'

'I haven't stolen anything!' Toyoo sobbed, as he began to understand the reason for the inquiry. 'The widow of a man named Agata gave me the sword, saying that it had belonged to her deceased husband. Please summon her, and she will explain that it's all a mistake.'

'There has been no one in our service by the name of Agata,' said the deputy, growing more angry. 'Lying will only make your punishment harsher.'

'When you've arrested me and have me at your mercy,' said Toyoo, 'how can I lie? I beg of you, please call the woman and ask her.'

Turning to the warriors, the deputy sputtered, 'Where is this Agata no Manago's house? Make the prisoner show you, and arrest the woman.'

The warriors acknowledged the command and forced Toyoo to lead them to Manago's palace, but when the troop arrived there, Toyoo discovered that the once-imposing pillars of the entrance were rotted, and most of the tiling had fallen and lay smashed, and from the eaves dense *shinobu* grass hung down, altogether lending the place an appearance of being deserted. Toyoo stood utterly dumbfounded at the sight, while warriors ran about rounding up the people in the immediate neighbourhood, and presently an old woodcutter, a rice-pounder, and others assembled, bowing down in fear.

'Who lives in this house?' the captain demanded of them. 'Is it true that this dwelling belongs to the wife of a man by the name of Agata?'

'I have never heard of a person by such a name,' replied an old smith, coming forward and kneeling. 'Until three years ago a man named Suguri used to reside here in very prosperous circumstances, and then he sailed to Tsukushi with a shipload of merchandise. The vessel was lost, and his family, which he had left behind in the house, were scattered, and since then no one has lived here. But yesterday the man accompanying you entered the property and stayed there for quite a while, as the old lacquer-maker told me, thinking it very suspicious.'

'In that case,' said the captain, 'search the house thoroughly, so we can report to the deputy,' Pushing the gate open, the warriors entered, and proceeding inside they found that the dwelling itself was in even greater ruin than the exterior. They advanced to the main quarters, and in the spacious garden, once magnificently landscaped, they saw a dried-up pond with a few withered water plants, and in the tangled thickets, which had grown wild, a large pine tree lay sprawled, toppled by the wind—a most desolate sight. As the warriors opened the shutters to the main hall, a foul stench came forth, overcoming all who were present and causing them to fall back in horror. Toyoo watched, speechless and with heavy heart.

Among the warriors, one named Kose no Kumagashi, a brave and robust soul, shouted, 'Come, men, follow me!' and tramping with a loud clatter across the floor boards, he charged forward. A full inch of dust lay accumulated, and rat feces were scattered everywhere. Amid the ruins there hung curtains behind which sat a young lady, as still and lovely as a lotus-blossom.

'The governor of the province summons you,' Kamugashi, facing the woman. 'Come at once!'

She gave no answer, and just as he advanced nearer, intending to seize her, a clap of thunder resounded; before they had any chance to move, everyone was suddenly thrown to the ground as if the earth were rent. No sooner had this happened than the woman vanished without a trace. On the floor lay a glittering heap, which the warriors approached with the utmost caution and examined. They found it to contain objects such as Korean brocades, Chinese damask, twill bands, shields, halberds, quivers, and hoes—all part of the sacred treasure stolen from the shrine. After the warriors had taken these things back with them and explained in detail about the strange happenings, both the deputy and the head priest realised that this was the work of the supernatural. They therefore sentenced Toyoo leniently, though he could not avoid being charged with the actual crime. He was remanded to the provincial office and cast into jail, but Tarō and his father were able to purchase his freedom, and following one hundred days' confinement, Toyoo was released. 'After what has happened, I'm ashamed to be seen around home,' he said to his father. 'May I visit elder sister in Yamato and stay at her place for a while?'

'Yes,' replied the father. 'Having gone through such a dreadful ordeal, there's some danger of your falling seriously ill. Go, and stay for several months,' and he provided him with an escort.

Toyoo's sister lived in the town of Tsuba Market, where she had married a merchant named Tanabe no Kanatada. The couple welcomed Toyoo's visit and were sympathetic about his recent experience. 'Remain with us just as long as you wish,' Tanabe said, treating him with warm hospitality. The New Year came, and then the Second Month.

Near Tsuba Market stood the Hase temple. Among the various Buddhist deities in Japan, the Goddess of Mercy of Hase had worked so many miracles that her renown had spread abroad to China. From the capital, as well as the countryside, many pilgrims journeyed to the temple. In the spring they were especially numerous, and these worshippers always sought lodging in Tsuba Market. Therefore, the town boasted of many inns to accommodate these travellers, and because the Tanabes' house sold such items as incense, holy lamps, and wicks, their shop always bustled with people coming and going. One day, a beautiful lady and her maidservant appeared among the patrons. They were dressed as though on an incognito pilgrimage from the capital. 'Look, our master is here!' said the maid, noticing Toyoo. Stunned with surprise, Toyoo saw that it was Manago and Maroya, and uttering a cry of terror, he fled inside to conceal himself.

'What's the matter?' asked Kanetada and his wife.

'Those demons have followed me here. Don't go near them!' he said, frantically trying to find a place to hide, as everyone got excited and began asking, 'Where?'

'Please, there is nothing to grow alarmed at,' said Manago as she entered. 'Don't be afraid, husband dear. It pained me bitterly to discover that I was responsible for your being accused of a crime, and I tried to find out where you had gone, so that I might explain things and put your mind at ease. I searched everywhere, and now that at last I've found you, I'm very happy. Listen to me, and think about what I say. If there were anything odd about me, do you imagine that I would appear in such a crowd of people and on such a lovely, calm day? My clothing has seams, and when I stand in the sunlight I have a shadow. Think it all over and decide for yourself—but you must, I beg of you.'

'I still can't believe that you're human,' said Toyoo, gradually regaining control over himself. 'After I was arrested and the warriors took me to your place, it was utterly changed. You sat amid the broken-down and dilapidated ruins—the sort of lair one would expect a goblin to inhabit—until the warriors tried to capture you, and then suddenly thunder came from out of the clear blue sky and you vanished without a trace. I saw it with my own eyes. Now you have followed me here. What are you going to do? Get out of here, at once!'

'I can understand why you feel this way,' said Manago, beginning to weep. 'But first you should listen to my side of the story, too. After I heard that the authorities had summoned you, I talked the matter over with an old man who lived nearby and for whom I had earlier done some favours, and he soon made the house look dilapidated and abandoned. Maroya suggested the device of a thunderous noise when I was about to be arrested.

'Afterward, I found a ship and fled to Naniwa, but I wanted to learn what became of you and decided to place my trust in this temple. Here, where the twin fir trees stand, to my great joy we have miraculously met as if carried by the same swift waters. No doubt it was owing to the great power and compassion of the Goddess of Mercy of Hase. As for the sacred treasures, how could a woman possibly steal such things? Most likely, it was an evil deed that my former husband did. Please think it over and try to understand just a little bit how much I love you,' and as she finished speaking, she broke down and wept inconsolably.

Toyoo was still suspicious, but he felt pity for her and lacked the strength to press the matter any further. Moreover, Kanetada and his wife were impressed by the sense of Manago's argument, and seeing how truly feminine her manner was, they harboured no doubts at all.

'When we heard Toyoo's story, we thought of what fearful things can happen in this world,' they said to Manago, 'but we believe that in our day and age supernatural incidents are unlikely to occur. Because of your patient search and long vigil in looking for Toyoo we are happy to let you stay with us, even though he may refuse to believe you,' and they gave her lodging. During the next day or two Manago endeared herself to the Tanabes and did her best to get them to intercede with Toyoo. The couple was so warmly delighted at her strength of character that they finally persuaded Toyoo to consummate his marriage.

Day by day, Toyoo's feelings toward Manago grew warmer, and he came to love her and to admire her beauty as much as before. He promised eternal devotion and was sorry only that to enjoy their love they had to wait like the clouds that nightly form on Katsuragi's peaks and Mt. Takama and with the morning bells of Hase Temple release their rain.

Presently, the Third Month arrived, and Kanetada turned to Toyoo and his bride saying, 'Come, and let us make an excursion! Although going to Yoshino might not be as pleasant as visiting the capital, most people prefer it to the Kii area.

"Yoshino of lovely name" is magnificent in springtime. Mt. Mifune and the Natsumi River offer endless variety, and I'm sure you'll agree that it's the best season.'

'I'd like to,' answered Manago with a smile. 'It's the place about which they say,

When the good men of old,
Beheld it and saw it well . . .

And I've heard that even people from the capital regret it when they can't visit Yoshino. But ever since I was a small girl, being in crowded places or attempting long journeys on foot has always made me ill; so, much though it saddens me I'm afraid that I had better not go with you. I'd be grateful enough if you'd bring me back a souvenir from the mountains.'

'No doubt it's the walking that makes you so ill,' protested Kanetada and his wife. 'True, we have no carriage, but still we shall by no means even let you step on the ground. If you were to stay here, think of how much Toyoo would worry.'

'After brother and sister have spoken so persuasively,' Toyoo added, 'you must try to go, even though you don't feel up to it.'

Despite Manago's reluctance, the party set out, and although they saw many splendid people nothing could compare with Manago's exceptional beauty. Because Kanetada and his wife had close connections with a certain temple, they went there to pray. The abbot welcomed them, saying, 'This spring you are late in coming to worship. Cherry-blossom season is more than half over and the nightingale's song may have lost some of its clear tone, but never mind—I'll find a good man to escort you about.' He set for them a frugal evening meal.

On the next morning a heavy mist covered the sky, and as it began to clear one could look down from the high ground where the temple was situated and make out a number of scattered hermitages. The chirruping of the mountain birds sounded muffled and dim. Flowers and blooming trees abounded in great variety. The atmosphere in the mountain hamlet had an invigorating freshness. 'People on their first visit,' said the guide, 'usually enjoy the area around the cascades most, because it offers the greatest number of interesting sights,' and he invited them to set out in that direction, descending a winding path into the valley. In ancient times an emperor's pleasure-palace had stood here, and now they watched the young fish swim upstream as the waters dashed through a gorge amid the rock-strewn rapids; they were delighted with the beauty of the fishes' dappled forms.

The party spread out their boxed lunches and were enjoying themselves as they ate. Then, walking over the rocks there appeared an old man with hair that looked as if it were tangled hempen yarn. Nevertheless, he moved his limbs in a lithe and agile stride. Pausing beneath the cascade, he trained a penetrating stare on the picnickers, and noticing him, Manago and Maroya turned to avoid his gaze. But the old man continued to glare at them.

'How strange,' he said. 'You evil demons! Why must you bewitch people? How dare you remain right in front of my eyes?'

Upon his uttering these words, Manago and Maroya suddenly arose and leaped into the cascade. A spout of water ascended, as if to the sky, and the two women disappeared. Clouds engulfed the party and as though spilling black India ink brought down a torrential deluge of rain, while the old man led the shocked and confused people back to the hamlet. They crouched under the eaves of a poor hut, feeling more dead than alive, and the old man turned to Toyoo and said, 'When I looked carefully at your face, I saw that those supernatural creatures were tormenting you, and if I hadn't rescued you, it would surely have cost you your life. In future you must be more cautious.'

Toyoo, stricken with fear, respectfully bowed his head to the ground and explained from the beginning what had happened, pleading, 'I beg you to save me.'

'Yes, I understand,' said the old man. 'These evil creatures are aged serpents. Their nature is governed by lust. It is said that when they mate with a bull, they give birth to a unicorn, and when they cohabit with horses they produce dragon steeds. No doubt, they tricked you and began this dalliance because they found you fair to look upon. But in any case, since they have proven to be so stubborn, I am afraid that you may still lose your life should you fail to take proper precautions.'

Hereupon, Toyoo and his companions felt all the more confused and frightened, and making obeisance to the old man, they said, 'You must be a living god.'

'I am no god, to be sure,' said the old man with a smile. 'I am a priest of the Yamato Shrine, and my name is Tagima no Kibito. I shall be pleased to escort you back. Let us go,' and so saying he set out, with the others following behind.

The next day, Toyoo went to the village of Yamato to thank the old priest for his kindness, taking with him three rolls of Mino silk and two bales of Tsukushi cotton. 'Please free me from possession by these spirits,' he begged.

After accepting the gift, the old priest distributed the goods to the shrine attendants, without keeping any for himself, and he said to Toyoo, 'Those creatures took advantage of your fair looks and tempted you. But you, yourself, owing to a lack of courage and spirit, fell victim to their temporary form. From now on if you act like a man and try to attain a more tranquil heart you will not need to depend on my power in order to get rid of such evil spirits. With all your might make your heart peaceful.' The old man's sincerity left a deep impression on Toyoo, who felt as if awakening from a dream, and after profusely expressing his gratitude to the priest, he returned.

'Because I have failed to be true to my own self, I have allowed beasts to deceive me,' Toyoo said to Kanetada. 'I must learn my duty to my father and elder brother and stop taking advantage of your hospitality. I am grateful for all that you have done in my behalf, and I shall visit you again.' Thereafter, he went back to the province of Kii.

When they heard of the frightful events that had passed, his father, mother, Tarō, and his sister-in-law felt that Toyoo was not really to blame. But they were disturbed at the evil spirit's obstinacy. 'The trouble is probably that we have let you remain unmarried,' they said, coming to a decision. 'We shall find you a wife.'

In the hamlet of Shiba there lived a man known as Shiba no Shōji, head of the local manor. He had an only daughter, named Tomiko, who served as a palace girl at the Court, and requesting that she be excused from her employment, Shiba sent a matchmaker to the Ōya house and proposed that Toyoo become his son-in-law. Negotiations went well, and the betrothal date was set. In due course a messenger was dispatched to the capital to escort Tomiko home, and she returned with much joy.

Accustomed to serving in the great palace, where she had spent several years, Tomiko's manners were impeccable, her appearance splendid to behold, and when Toyoo moved to the Shibas' home and saw her, he felt satisfied in every way with her remarkable charm. But there was something about her that reminded him of his previous love for Manago. The first night passed without any event. On the second night, however, after Toyoo became slightly intoxicated, he said, 'Now that you have spent several years in service at the palace, we country folk must strike you as decidedly boorish. While you were in the capital what captains, imperial advisors, and the like did you sleep with? It's very disconcerting to think about!'

Although Toyoo had spoken playfully, Tomiko suddenly straightened up and replied, 'You, who have forgotten your old promises and have stooped to toy with a worthless common creature! It is your behaviour, on the contrary, that's disgusting.' Her appearance changed. The voice was unmistakably that of Manago.

Astonished to hear her, Toyoo was so struck with fear that his hair stood on end, and he knew not what to do. Noticing his consternation, Manago smiled and said, 'My dear, you mustn't be afraid. We have vowed to the oceans. We have pledged to the mountains. How can you forget so quickly, when it was ordained by fate that we should meet again. If you believe what other people say and recklessly try to abandon me, I shall seek vengeance, and tall though the peaks of the mountains of the Kii High Road may be, your blood will drain from the ridges into the valleys. You must not be so rash as to throw away your life in vain.'

Toyoo trembled uncontrollably, as a man confronted with the prospect of immediate death.

'My lord,' came a voice from behind the screen, 'why are you so upset? This should be an occasion for rejoicing,' and so saying, Maroya appeared.

Upon seeing her, Toyoo fell into a swoon. His eyes closed, and he lay face downward. Manago and Maroya tried cajolery. They tried threats. They tried to bring him around by speaking in turns, but he remained unconscious until the night ended.

Presently, he escaped from the sleeping chamber and went to his father-in-law, saying in a low voice for fear of being overheard, 'Something terrible has happened,' and after explaining he pleaded, 'What can we do about it? Please think of something.'

Shiba and his wife turned pale and lamented, 'But what can we do? There is, however, a priest from the Kurama temple, outside the capital, who every year makes a pilgrimage to Kumano, and since yesterday he has been staying at a cloister on a nearby mountain. He is a holy man who knows many kinds of exorcism and whose prayers have been eminently successful against plagues, locusts, and evil influence; people around here show him great respect. Let us consult with him.' Shiba lost no time in sending word, and the priest soon arrived.

After learning of what had come to pass, the priest, who was quite confident of himself, said, 'To capture these creatures that resort to witchcraft presents little difficulty. There's no need at all for you to worry.' He made it sound so simple that everyone felt relieved.

First, the priest asked for some sulphur. Then he mixed it with medicine water and placed the solution in a small flask. As he moved toward the sleeping chamber everyone recoiled in horror, but the priest laughed at them and said, 'All of you, old and young alike, wait here, and I'll catch the serpents and show them to you.'

No sooner did he open the door of the sleeping chamber than a demon thrust its head out at the priest. The projecting extremity was so huge that it filled the doorway, gleaming even whiter than newly fallen snow, with eyes like mirrors and horns like the bare boughs of a tree. The creature opened its mouth more than three feet wide; its crimson tongue darted, as if to swallow the priest in a single gulp.

'Horror!' cried the holy man, as he dropped the flask that he held in his hand. His legs no longer able to support him, he fell over backwards and crawled away, barely managing to escape.

'It's awful. The creature is a god of evil; my prayers are useless. If I hadn't got away on hands and knees, I'd surely have lost my life,' he said, losing consciousness. Shiba and the others tried to help him regain his senses, but poisonous vapours seemed to have attacked him. His face and body were mottled red and black, as though he were stained with dye, and he felt as hot to touch as a bonfire. Later, his eyes alone had power to move, and although it looked as if he wished to speak, he was unable to utter a sound. They kept sponging him with water, but in the end he died. Each of those who saw the priest pass away wailed in confusion and felt as if his own soul might depart from his body.

Toyoo eventually managed to pull himself together enough to say, 'Even the prayers of this most eminent priest have failed. Because the beasts pursue me with such tenacity, they'll seek me out as long as I remain flesh and blood. There is no use causing pain to others for the sake of my life alone. From now on I'll speak to you no more of this matter, and you mustn't worry,' and so saying, he went toward the sleeping chamber.

'Has the demon caused you to lose your mind?' asked his father- and mother-in-law. But paying no heed to them, Toyoo approached the room. Quietly, he entered.

Manago and Maroya sat facing one another. There was no sign of anything unusual.

'Whatever possessed you to ask someone to try to seize me?' said Manago, turning to Toyoo. 'If you ever again spitefully seek to get rid of us, not only will you give up your life, but I will also make certain that every person in this community shall come to grief. Be thankful rather over our constancy to you and, really, don't ever again behave in such a fickle way.'

Although Toyoo was now repelled by her affectionate tone, he replied, 'I have heard tell of a proverb that says, "Even if a man does not intend to injure a tiger, the beast may still attack the man." Your heart is not human. You've trapped me and brought me trouble again and again. It's frightful that our passing affair should lead you to be so vindictive. I understand that you love me the way a real person would, but why should we stay here and cause other people grief? You must at least spare Tomiko's life. Then you may take me anywhere.' Full of joy at hearing such words, Manago nodded in assent.

Arising and withdrawing from the room, Toyoo said to his father-in-law, 'The dreadful creatures will continue to follow me, and it would be heartless of me to remain here and bring you additional suffering. If you will let me go, I think that you will no longer find your daughter's life to be in danger.'

Shiba, however, was adamant in his refusal, saying, 'My ancestors were warriors, I'll have you know, and I'd be ashamed of what your father's family would think, should I act so spinelessly. I have a better idea. In Komatsubara, at the Dōjōji temple, there lives a revered and venerated priest named Abbot Hōkai. I've heard that old age prevents him from going abroad, but should I ask him, he won't let me down,' and the father-in-law hurried off at once on horseback.

Owing to the long way, it was already the middle of the night before Shiba reached the temple. The old abbot crawled out of the monastery's sleeping quarters, and after listening to the story, he said, 'Yes, it does sound dreadful. I am now rather forgetful—I hardly remember how to work my cures, but I could never ignore a misfortune in your house! You go back now, and I'll come later.' He brought out a monk's robe, which had been saturated in mustard-seed incense, and gave it to Shiba, saying, 'Gently lure one of the beasts to you. Then take this cloak and throw it swiftly over her head and hold the garment down with all your might. If you show the slightest weakness, they are quite likely to escape. Keep your wits about you,' he concluded, 'and do your task well.'

Shiba was delighted as he mounted his horse and galloped home. Secretly, he called Toyoo and gave him the monk's robe and said, 'Carefully do as Abbot Hōkai instructed.' Hiding the garment inside his clothing, Toyoo went to the sleeping chamber.

'Father has given us permission to leave. Come, let us depart at once,' he said, and taking advantage of Manago's pleasure over the idea, he drew out the monk's robe, cast it over her and held it down with all his strength.

'Stop! You're hurting me,' Manago shouted. 'How can you be so heartless. Let me go!' But Toyoo pressed down even harder, exerting his full power, and soon afterward Abbot Hōkai arrived by palanquin. The servants helped him to alight and showed him to the chamber, where he intoned prayers in a solemn chant. At last, he told Toyoo to step back.

Abbot Hōkai removed the robe, and there lay Tomiko, unconscious, with a white serpent more than three feet in length coiled motionlessly on her breast. The old abbot picked up the snake and put it in an iron urn, which his disciple held. He recited additional prayers, and from behind the screen there crawled a small serpent about a foot long, which he also placed in the urn. Thereupon, he took the incensed robe, fastened it tightly around the urn, and departed in his palanquin as everyone clasped hands and wept profusely, paying their respects to the holy man.

After returning to the temple, Abbot Hōkai ordered a deep pit to be dug in front of the main hall, and he commanded that the urn be buried for all time to prevent the spirits' further appearance on earth. It is said that the serpents' mound remains to this day.

According to tradition, Shiba's daughter, Tomiko, never recovered and eventually died, but Toyoo lived on in good health.

Preproduction:
The Script

Yoshikata Yoda offers one of the most comprehensive biographical studies of Mizoguchi available in Japanese. As the director's devoted scriptwriter for many years, Yoda is uniquely qualified to offer insights into Mizoguchi's own gift for screenwriting. One chapter of Yoda's book, *Mizoguchi Kenji: Hito to Geijutsu* (Kenji Mizoguchi: His Life and Art), consists of a letter Mizoguchi wrote to him while the script was in progress. Yoda acknowledges that Mizoguchi chose this method of communication because he feared that his scriptwriter might misunderstand his intention during the course of conversation. I have included Joanne Bernardi's translation of the entire letter, which appears as an appendix to her thesis on Yoda's original screenplay. The letter is fragmented and hasty, yet it shows how Mizoguchi thought about work in progress. Frequently Mizoguchi apologizes for his blunt criticism. Yoda wryly notes that Matsutaro Kawaguchi, who collaborated on early drafts of the *Ugetsu* script, believed the director's apology really meant: "You idiots! Can't you figure this out for yourselves?"

Letter from Kenji Mizoguchi to
His Scriptwriter Yoshikata Yoda

*First title:
Origin of the work. A paragraph. While the authors of this film read *Ugetsu Monogatari* with great enjoyment, various images came to mind. Although this movie is perhaps quite different from the original work, it conveys these images, which still linger on. For this reason, we have entitled the film *Ugetsu Monogatari*.

*Please put this into fine prose.

*What follows the first title "When the snow melts . . ." sounds a little presumptuous. It will be incomprehensible to people seeing the film for the first time.

*Please put the name "Shibata" into the next title. What I said about the first title also follows here.

*In the village:
"I'll kill you!" Some movement of weapons should accompany this line.

*I think it would be a good idea to kill off one of the fleeing men—in front of one of the houses along the road.

*Judging from what has come before, it is unnatural for Tōbei not to be caught and pressed into service just because he wants to become a samurai.

*It doesn't look right if he doesn't escape, or do something, when he is about to be carried off.

*In the backyard:
The line "It sounds like the battle's beginning" is ludicrous when you think about

From "Ugetsu Monogatari ni Tsuite no Tegami," in *Mizoguchi Kenji no Hito to Geijutsu* by Yoda Yoshikata (Tokyo: Tabata Shoten, 1970), pp. 214–227. Yoda's book was first published in 1964 by Eiga Geijutsu Sha; before publication, portions of the book were serialized in *Eiga Geijutsu,* between 1961 and 1964. This letter first appeared in the February 1963 issue.

[Excerpts of the letter have been published before, by Michel Mesnil as "Lettres sur le scenario des *Contes de la lune vague*," in his book *Mizoguchi Kenji* (Paris: Éditions Seghers, 1965, pp. 113–122); by Peter Morris, in the monograph *Mizoguchi Kenji* (Ottawa: Canadian Film Institute, 1967, pp. 14–20); and by Leonard Schrader, in the chapter on Mizoguchi in his unpublished manuscript "The Masters of Japanese Film," available from the Pacific Film Archives. Morris's English translation appears to have been done from Mesnil's text, which contains many errors. Schrader's translation is very similar to Morris's, although his English is occasionally more comprehensible. None of the three translations seems as reliable as Joanne Bernardi's.—Editor's note] it. Instead the sense that the battle has already begun somewhere off in the distance should be conveyed.

*It might be a good idea to insert an attack and a fire during the night, before the backyard scene. It would intensify the sense of terror. Then this terror would be present in the feelings of the two characters in the scene.

*The mountain path:
Don't restrict the action to the main characters. Use others as well.

*On the mountain:
"I want to make my fortune!" Think of a good line that implies more than just money—

—Regarding the word "honor": Think of the relationship between honor and social status. Look for a word that might clearly communicate this sense to the audience.

*My personal opinions:
As we discussed several times before, I think that at this point we should depict the feelings of the masses toward war. When the two characters talk about this battle being a struggle between Hashiba and Shibata for Oichinokata[1]—about Hashiba and Shibata being powerful men, and about the violence toward the people—I think it would be relevant to have one of the main characters join in on their gossip; but give the bulk of the dialogue to the minor characters. Study this.

*My opinions on the script up to the scene in the boat:

*Violence that takes the name of war due to the public or private interests of those in power—what physical and spiritual torment this must be for the common people! Yet even under these conditions the people must continue to live, they must eat. (I want to emphasize this as the theme of the film up to this point. What do you think?)

*Genjūrō's backyard:
The line about loading the cart before the battle begins—This sounds too much like explanatory dialogue on the part of the author. Since a line that implies the sense of "battle" is all that is necessary, try to write something that would be natural for a craftsman to say.
I'm not referring to this phrase alone, we had dialogue like this in the previous draft. I think this is a serious problem that destroys the cohesiveness of the drama.

---

1. Oichi was the younger sister of Oda Nobunaga, the wife of Asai Nagamasa, and the mother of Hideyoshi's favorite mistress, Yodogimi. Oichi is believed to have been a great beauty.

I've read this far for tonight. This is what I would like:

*Synthesize all the individual details.

*Reinforce everything up to here. Find a backbone.

*Feel free to make these adjustments yourself.

*I think I would like to have a poem in the boat scene. Perhaps something with the nostalgic flavor of Hagiwara Sakutarō.[2]

*Miyagi's speech to her son at the foot of the mountains—the bit about war. When I read it I had the feeling the battle was already at its height, but since you had the same line once before, the drama seems to go backwards. For some reason these lines Miyagi says to her son really bother me. Her speech is very trite. Study this.

*The word "*zappi*" [or *zōhi,* low-ranking foot soldier] sounds better than "*damono*" [low-ranking foot soldier]. Think carefully of words that communicate to the audience. "*Sue*" [porcelain] is the same.

*The man:
I'd like you to have him say "water, water." Then, since no water is at hand, have them give him sake.

*The word "*kassen*" [battle] sounds Chinesey, and seems like something coined by a Meiji official. Isn't there a simple Japanese word that is easily accessible to the audience?

*The argument whether to turn the ship back, or to go forward:
Carefully restudy this problem from the viewpoint of both the dialogue and the drama, in order to save the scene from becoming mere exposition. Emphasize the emotion.

**Please restudy the structure of the scene on the lake.

*The beach at Onoe:
In this scene too, be careful not to turn the conversation into narration. Emphasize emotion without being too excessive.

*The latter part of the boat scene, the parting on the beach:
Work on this so that it does not seem stereotyped or banal.

*The sequence following Ohama from Sakamoto to the road is fine. However, please don't make the dialogue, which is intended to reinforce the action, seem like narration.

---

2. Hagiwara Sakutarō (1886–1942) was a major poet noted for his evocative use of colloquial language.

*A request:
Reading the script this far I see no indication of either the psychological or emotional makeup of the individual characters in the boat. Give me drama and poetry—I am probably asking for too much, but please show me in some sort of diagram the interrelation of these elements.

*The phrasing of the first title is a little blunt. It resembles proletarian literature.

*If you indicate the places of labor in the beginning, and show fields, paddies, forests, etc. for farmers and workrooms for craftsmen, it would be a good idea to follow a structure that plays off these locations—for example, mother, wife, a farewell scene between parent and child, all in the place of labor.

*(In reference to this, I feel it would be appropriate to indicate Genjūrō's workplace.)

*The comparison between the early battle scenes and the scenes in the places of labor:
The workplace is tranquil. The evening meal is also tranquil. There is nothing overtly dramatic about these scenes, but if they are passed off as exposition they will lack some sort of climax and end up completely devoid of drama. As director, I would find it difficult to deal with such scenes as they would not conform to the continuity—it would be like oil in water.

*The scene on the clearing on the mountain is also expository. It would be more dramatic if you showed, for example, a child crying from hunger.

The continuity of what you showed me the other day was confused. I am worried that we might have a problem with the beginning ending up as mere exposition. Study this.

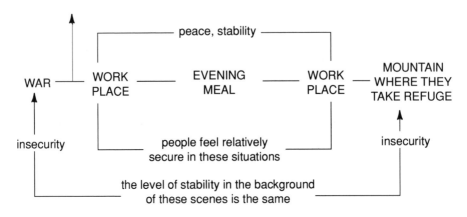

*I believe various partial dramatic climaxes are necessary to the basic line of narrative.

*In order to eliminate explanatory dialogue, try to create a drama that generates from the characters.

*An opinion after reading this far: Excuse me for saying this after only going through it once, but each character's reaction to war, as depicted on screen, seems farcical and trite. I apologize.

*I remember something I heard in China, which you are also familiar with:
While the soldiers were busy shooting at each other the peasant women looked on in disdain, and continued to go about washing their laundry in the stream.

*In this particular scene I detect a certain depth of human feeling, and an awesome terror.

*You're being old-fashioned. For one thing, in order to make characters that are not artificial, it is essential for the author to observe people outside the framework of both his and the director's own experience or predetermined ideas. Don't follow the trite paths others have traveled before. I think it is important to discover something new that others have not yet become aware of.
This method of careful observation gives freshness and vitality to the work—I feel like I'm preaching to Buddha.

*I think the plot and characters are stereotyped.

*In depicting human personality:
There are talkative people, reticent people, ornery people, polite people, people who fake politeness, people who are foolish but pretend to be wise, or who are wise but pretend to be foolish.

*All the characters' responses are the same length. If the writer arranges the lines too cautiously the dialogue will become too explanatory.

*Regarding Miyagi's feelings toward her native village: Her parents are buried there. There are fields and rice paddies that have been passed down by her ancestors from generation to generation, and there is the constant changing of the seasons year after year. People live and die on the same land. All this must be added to her affection for her husband.

*In the first part of the scene on the lake:
I don't want explanatory dialogue, I want poetry. The last part of the scene is a little ridiculous, too.

*In the dialogue here, too, if someone says something it absolutely must be answered.

*A boat that has been attacked by pirates should float by more than once; one boat should have just a dead body in it.

A quiet eerieness—I'd like to keep the second time the boat goes by just as it is in the script.

*The farewell scene at the boat seems too noisy—too typical.

*Niwa Nagahide kō:
Didn't the title "*kō*" [lord] come into use after Meiji? "*Sama*" [lord, marquis, *daimyō*] is better.

*I'd like the dialogue to be in modern Japanese, yet still give a sense of the period.

*I like the scenes in Sakamoto, but on second reading the atmosphere and dialogue seem superficial. The drama needs to be fleshed out.

*Do some research on Niwa Nagahide.

*Since it would be very expensive to show Niwa himself departing for the front, I think we could imply his departure by showing a vanguard of troops, commanders, and private soldiers.

*You could re-create the atmosphere of an inn of that period by filming a part of an old temple. The disorder will give an impression of the confusion of war (the idea that so many refugees have come to the town that they are obliged to take temporary refuge at the temple).

*I think the word "*ito*" [thread] is too contemporary. How about the word "*kinu*" [silk] or the name of a prized silk of that period, "*neriginu*" [glossed silk].

*Regarding Tōbei's petition to get to the front:
Instead of what you wrote—having him sell himself—I think one way to get him in with the soldiers is to have him tell a pack of lies, like "I am the notorius monk so-and-so of Hieizan" or "I am the master so-and-so of this or that manor," as if he were someone who has accomplished great deeds. Look into this.

*Tsuji:[3]
We'll have the administration work out the location fees; also I'd like the final draft of the script to include a description of the arrangement of the cups.

*Regarding the foreshadowing and interpretation of the lead-in from reality to symbolism:
When Miyagi prays a sign appears—how about something like a phantom ship?

*The way the ghost appears seems too realistic. The previous reference to Rokujō is fine, but here, can't you have the spirit appear in such a way that it leads the characters into a dream-like poetry? Think about this.

---

3. Tsuji Hisakazu was the associate producer of *Ugetsu*. Yoda's note: ". . . after this Tsuji collaborated with Mizoguchi on the production of the director's subsequent works."

*If this is a departed spirit, what Miyagi later becomes is an apparition. Think of ways in which we can make this distinction.

*Regarding the departed spirit and passion:
Haven't you got a good idea? I'll also look around in books. There should be something in drama involving ghosts.

*I haven't attempted a ghost story for several decades.[4] Please do your utmost to create a well-defined atmosphere and expression of feelings. I will also look into this.

*The devolution of the drama flows well up to this point, and I think it is quite good.

*Regarding the scenes of Miyagi after the ghost story subplot:
What do you think about making these scenes more pathetic in order to contrast them to the preceding ghost tale? Look into this. I am anxious to have contrast in order to perfect the drama.

*Another opinion after reading this far:
Try to develop the dialogue from prosaically conversational to realistically dramatic.

*Pillage and violence:
What do you think about showing some looting of neighborhood houses in Ohama's first scene in their mountain dwelling?

*I would like to talk to you about Kyō Machiko's aura of perfume and incense.

*To explain the three women in terms of their fragrance:
Miyagi—a commonplace fragrance, the musty smell of the family altar
Ohama—the plentiful smoldering of cheap incense in a cemetery in the fields
Wakasa—the perfume and incense you smell in a dubious four-and-a-half–mat room in a cheap assignation house—or in a lavatory (I think this is really a very strange smell).

At this juncture you could try out various possibilities by smelling a variety of fragrances—we can do nothing unless you try this, even if it doesn't develop into anything useful.

*The resolution of the Wakasa subplot is very interesting.

*Your attempt to make the on-screen presentation of the Mephisto character Yozaemon is an extremely delicate matter. I'm stumped, but I'll think about it some more. If you have any good ideas, go ahead with them.

---

4. Mizoguchi is referring to his *Kyoren no Onna Shishō* (Passion of a Woman Teacher, 1926), for which Matsutarō Kawaguchi wrote his first script for Mizoguchi.

**Concerning our telephone conversation:

*Regarding the ghost story subplot about Wakasa:
How should we treat this story?
1. as a ghost story that is contemporary, real;
2. as a mystical, supernatural tale in which a spirit appears—this would involve ironic overtones on the part of the writer;
3. as a story that is neither realistic nor mystical.

In any case no matter how we do it there will be too many realistic elements that come up in Wakasa's subplot. We must try to balance the subplot with the consistent realism of the main story line, and keep the two from becoming like water and oil.

*The ominous eeriness of the encounter with the ransacked boat on the lake foreshadows the following turn of events. It should be followed up by repeated indications of this atmospheric weirdness in order to preserve continuity. This is vital, so think carefully about how to arrange it. I have no plan at the moment. If we discuss it, we're sure to come up with something.

*The mountain village of Shiozu:

*These are farmers. It is illogical to have someone being captured "upstairs."

*It bothers me not to have the previous draft on hand, but have you amply expressed Miyagi's feelings while she wanders in search of shelter, waiting for her husband who does not return?

*The arrangement of these scenes is too predictable. Work on the psychological makeup of Miyagi, Tōbei, and the other characters. We cannot have the dramatic action dwindle to mere plot.

*I've chosen the vehicle of a ghost story because I cannot adequately handle this subject matter in a realistic, contemporary drama; also, as a method of expression that has ironic overtones, it is conducive to the presentation of a historical perspective that reveals something about society. It would be useless to use this vehicle to make a mere curiosity piece.

*The scene where Miyagi is dragged away, and Ohama's rape scene:
It seems like the same technique has been used in both scenes. Both involve a house and two people. Please revise.

*The sequence with Miyagi in the official's residence:
This scene is preceded by pathetic scenes involving Miyagi, and followed by a cut-back to Genjūrō's success. As a result the plot seems overly self-conscious, like the plots of so many other scripts. Discard this technique and probe into the psychological aspects that are at the core of the narrative.

*From this point on the script must concentrate on the theme, and it should carefully reveal the context of the drama to the audience. Make a clear and sober statement that reflects your ideas about the emotions and psychology involved.

*The sudden gust of wind in the prison scene is characteristic of Son Wu Kong.[5] I hesitate to include something like this.

*The sequence inside the house on the temple grounds:
This sequence becomes increasingly important. It should not be used merely to reveal Wakasa's identity. If we wish to elaborate on the supernatural aspects of Wakasa's psychology we must give more thought to the manner of the presentation as well as to other internal aspects of the narrative. Work on it.

*I don't think the audience would be satisfied with that technique either.

*This latter half of the narrative is more important than the first half. From this point on the theme, ideas, or whatever is communicated is most important.

*The scene with the man called "Aradera Yoza"—isn't he killed in the same way as Mokuami's god of death? What the writer is trying to satirize through this character is unclear—it is not fully developed. It is too convenient to the point of being hackneyed.

*From this sequence on both the form and content are ponderous. The audience will be squirming in their seats. This has been handled very crudely. There is too much exposition. If there is no dramatic spontaneity, the narrative will lose all vigor. Think about this carefully. I apologize.

*The scenes in Sakamoto:
I get the feeling the writer is frantically trying to keep up with the events. Give me action and depiction weighty with substance. If it is too light there will be no preparation for the appearance of the mysterious spirit, Wakasa. I agree with the use of fades and irises here,[6] but something that gives us a sense of Sakamoto should have emerged before this section.

I find it hard to accept the warm welcome given the victorious soldiers. In my imagination I see only a village darkened by sadness—the gloom of wartime disaster.

*This is a rude observation, but having read this far I feel the various events and threads of narrative have taken the shape of a historical narrative. Interesting is

5. The protagonist in *Xi-you ji* (Journey to the West), a sixteenth-century Chinese supernatural novel based on a celebrated legend.
6. The terms used here are "*bokashi*" (a wipe, vignette, or fade transition) and "*shibori*" (an iris-in or iris-out transition).

interesting, but the ideology (ugly word) with which we approached this film is vital in preserving the integrity of the drama. I apologize.

*Scenes in the brothel:
These scenes are also explanatory and roughly drawn. They sound crude. Regarding Ohama's entrance—we can't give the impression that she's some sort of bustling chambermaid type. (I understand that you must be exhausted, and I am incensed that the company so avariciously measures our time.)

*Ohama:
The scene where she meets up with Tōbei corresponds to the scene in the Maupassant story where the man from the hospital goes to visit. Appreciate the way the visit is handled in the original, and study it carefully—the man's conscience, his goodness. Your observation of human nature is important here (I am exaggerating all of this a bit). Then it will not seem abrupt or artificial. Arrange the scenes before and after so that what you want to emphasize is made very clear. No matter how long the scenes are they will still engage the viewer. If we do not handle this sequence well we might as well not have a script. Give me striking scenes. I'm relying on you to put this together carefully. I apologize.

*The brothel:
Show Ohama's feelings toward Tōbei. The nature of her identity as a woman. The writer's portrayal of Ohama should be of a woman with a good-natured, down-to-earth quality (in doing this, aren't we also portraying the situation of the common people in the face of tragedy?).

Express this. The spirituality of human love. These are pretentious words but the writer has been building up to this. (I understand you are short on time, but isn't it pedantic to just go through the motions?) As director, I'd like to know your considered opinion of this. I apologize.

*There is no need for Genjūrō to be with Ohama—Tōbei alone is enough. The two of them can exchange some dramatic dialogue. I strongly feel this is necessary. The drama will arise from the situation.

*After the lake scene:
As they row out across the lake Genjūrō must be feeling very emotional. The idea of a lifelong separation from his wife and child—this human aspect is necessary.

Reviews and
Commentaries

Reviews

As was described in the introduction to this volume, the critical reception when *Ugetsu* was first released in Japan could be called at best indifferent. One exception was Ichiro Ueno, who treats the film as a major work and recognizes Mizoguchi's meticulous attention to detail and his ability to synthesize the disparate elements of the film in an aesthetically compelling way. Ueno is certainly the first critic to refer to the film as a "masterpiece."

Western responses to the film are presented chronologically because *Ugetsu* was released at different times in different countries. Reviewers in the West were undoubtedly influenced by the film's great success at the prestigious Venice Film Festival and by a contemporary rush of interest in Japanese film (*Rashomon*—and Kurosawa—had been discovered in the West in 1952). American reviews in 1954 were almost uniformly laudatory, and not just in specialized film journals. Bosley Crowther, the influential critic for the *New York Times,* was clearly uncertain about the film ("strange," "weird," and "esoteric," are characteristic words in his commentary), but he was undoubtedly impressed. The *Motion Picture Herald,* a trade newspaper, praised the film, despite its lack of the commercial possibilities the paper usually values. *Time* emphasized Ugetsu's introspective beauty, stressing qualities rare in Western films.

By the time the film was being shown in France (1959) and in Britain (1962) Mizoguchi had died, but his work was becoming more widely known, at least to serious students of film. Both Eric Rohmer and Penelope Gilliat had no hesitation in calling *Ugetsu* a masterpiece and in comparing the director's films with various major texts of both film and literature in the Western tradition. However, some reviewers, especially those like Paul Rotha who were committed to verisimilitude in film, found *Ugetsu*'s mixture of fantasy and realism "sadly undistinguished."

Kinema Jumpo
Ichiro Ueno

F irst of all, I am impressed by the film's authentic quality. As always, Mizoguchi has paid minute attention to every aspect of the work at hand. He has
taken special care with photography, music, lighting, and period authenticity—aspects of production apt to be treated matter-of-factly by other directors.
But Mizoguchi brings a distinctive tone to every element, ensuring that each
contributes to the overall effect he desired to achieve in *Ugetsu*.

As a synthetic art form, film should always aspire to achievements like *Ugetsu*.
Very few Japanese films apart from Mizoguchi's accomplish anything like this
perfect synthesis. (Ozu's works may also be considered synthetic, but his integration of all the elements involved is nowhere as whole, as thorough, as in Mizoguchi's films.)

Mizoguchi's stylistic perfectionism derives from his obsession with fitting all
parts into a perfect whole. There is more than mere fastidiousness at work here. I
respect Mizoguchi's efforts to make a film as a whole suit its subject matter to its
mode of expression, and I also admire his expertise in bringing just this perfect
harmony to *Ugetsu*. By all means, I should also mention the excellence of his
collaborators: Kazuo Miyagawa for cinematography, Fumio Hayasaka for music
owing so much to (traditional) Japanese instruments; Kisaku Ito for art direction
of scenes involving the Kutsuki mansion, and Kusune Kainosho for management
of civil war period authenticity. . . .

The film begins when Genjuro loads bundles of pottery onto a cart, assisted by
his wife Miyagi (played by Kinuyo Tanaka). Tobei, ambitious to become a
samurai, goes along on the selling trip, ignoring his wife Ohama's attempt to stop
him. Though their pottery is sold, Tobei, who does not possess a suit of armor, is
rejected by soldiers. Around this point, we notice that the tempo of the film picks
up. Then, it slows for the scenes in the Kutsuki mansion. This matching of pace
and event in *Ugetsu* is a new structural device in Mizoguchi films. Because
Mizoguchi deals with a story set in time of war, this smooth pacing of events (until
the scenes in the Kutsuki mansion) helps create a sense of urgency.

Genjuro, who has decided to capitalize on the war, begins to bake more pottery,
aided by Tobei. The Shibata army arrives and ransacks the village. Here, the
reality of war takes on more vivid detail, continuing to function as background.
Even so, Mizoguchi's treatment of war is not really successful. The actual spe-

From *Kinema Jumpo* no. 62 (15 April 1953): 54–55. Copyright © 1953 by Ichiro Ueno. Translated by
Keiko I. McDonald for this volume. A section devoted to literary sources for *Ugetsu* is deleted since
many other critics have covered this aspect. Also left out is a synopsis of some important scenes.

cifics of war's chaos does not harmonize with the fantastic realm which predominates in the second half.

Genjuro and Tobei, together with their wives, load merchandise on a boat and set out to cross Lake Biawa. The shooting of this scene was done on a set; the boat with low sounds of oars moves into the mist hovering over the quiet lake; then, a deserted boat comes floating into view. This scene is charged with a mysterious aura, and is an exquisite example of synthesis of all aspects of production: photography, lighting, music, and directing. . . .

Tobei, who has profited from his business, buys a suit of armor and becomes a samurai as he wished. Ohama, who has lost sight of him, is kidnapped by soldiers and raped in a dilapidated temple. This event is rather abrupt, but the impersonal and sharp portrayal offers Mizoguchi-like mastery.

Genjuro, who has been separated from Tobei and Ohama, meets a beautiful princess (played by Machiko Kyo) and her old attendant (played by Kikue Mori). At their request, he delivers pottery to their residence, the Kutsuki mansion. Here we are introduced to the main theme of the film. When the party of three enters the ruined gate, and goes through the garden overgrown with weeds, suddenly the vista of a deserted samurai mansion opens up. The effect of this transition is exquisite. In this mansion, Genjuro, entertained by the great beauty, forgets his home and family. The way Kyo, cast as a ghost, Kikue Mori, and two ladies-in-waiting move reflects the conventions of No. Makeup, lowered heads, and movements of legs and arms are all conscious borrowings from No formalism, whose prescribed pattern of acting is successful in creating a peculiar kind of fantasy. The scene of the Kutsuki mansion will doubtless endure as a classic. If I were allowed to ask for more, it would be for a little more thrill of horror. Moreover, Masayuki Mori's acting needs more of the ghostliness one would expect from someone haunted by the spirit of a dead person. However, Machiko Kyo's posture as a noble lady is successful, and Kikue Mori is equally adept at creating a devilish mood when she closes in on Genjuro. . . .

Mood, which is Mizoguchi's hallmark, permeates the film, and we can safely call *Ugetsu* a masterpiece. However, I do regret that the fantastic and real realms do not blend harmoniously. The disharmony may derive from Mizoguchi's desire to modernize the film's storyline too much. Contrary to the director's intention, I get the impression that the tragedy he explores is not caused by war, but by human ambition. After all, Mizoguchi is the director *par excellence* of deeply felt emotions.

As for acting, Masayuki Mori and Kinuyo Tanaka have done considerably well, though neither is especially outstanding. Sakae Ozawa, too conscious of his role, is a little superficial in acting. Though she is not in the forefront, Mitsuko Mito is good at expressing the ardent wish of a wife who tries to curb her husband's ambition. However, her performance as a prostitute falls short, partly because her character in the scenario is not fully developed. On the whole, all the cast is talented.

New York Times
Bosley Crowther

The prospect of Japanese movies ever building up to the point where they equal TV as competition to the domestic circulation of American films is one that the Hollywood producers need not view with alarm. Indeed, it does not appear likely that Japanese pictures will prove as much of a threat as did mahjong. And we say this with no disparagement of the few that have been seen here since the war or disregard of the swath they have been cutting these past few years in the film festivals abroad.

It is simply that Japanese movies, such as the beautiful "Rashomon," which broke the post-war hiatus a couple of years ago, and now the frenetic "Ugetsu," which arrived at the Plaza last week, are so different in their concepts and structures from the general characteristics of American films that the average patron of pictures is sure to find them as baffling as their speech. And we hasten to add that we say this with no disparagement meant towards the average patron of pictures, who has a very good right to be confused.

For the very Japanese culture from which these pictures spring is one that evolves in symbolisms, innuendoes, and subtle moods quite unlike the forms of factual expression that are native to American thinking and films. The mind and the emotions are excited by devices of aesthetic form, fantasy, and suggestion, which are much more delicate than the devices that we're accustomed to.

Allusive

"Rashomon" was a perfect evidence of it. This brilliant, allusive tale of the total reactions of three people to a violence committed in a woods, was steeped in a cultural climate so misty and rarefied that an awareness of what was happening in the picture was not at all easy to perceive. The effort to do so was worth it, for the delight of realization that arrived as the philosophical concept gained clarity was quite apart from any such we usually know.

And the same is true with "Ugetsu"—although we must say the realization here is neither as profound or fascinating as it was in "Rashomon." The story here is of two peasants in sixteenth-century Japan—in a time of great warfare and pillage—who are consumed by ambition and greed. One peasant wants to be wealthy, the other wants to be a samurai, a mighty warrior, bent upon conquest. Both are shown the folly of their dreams.

From the *New York Times* (12 September 1954).

The peasant who wants to be wealthy is lured into a blissful affair with a beautiful, fragile princess who turns out to be a ghost. And the one who wants to be a warrior gets a brief spell of triumph through a fraud, during which his neglected wife is captured by other warriors and made a prostitute.

This, we say, is the story that finally emerges through the gauze of weird, restless, imagistic action—violent, contorted scenes of struggling peasants and soldiers; strange, dreamy episodes of love in the exquisite house of the princess; vague, melancholy interludes. Music appropriate to the strangeness of the images points the eerie moods. At times it is very difficult to fathom remotely what goes.

No "Teahouse"

But the sensuous details are intriguing, the acting is hypnotically formalized—especially that of Machiko Kyo, the ghostly princess, who was the wife in "Rashomon"—and the whole composition of it is a challenge for the student of films. Don't expect anything as literal as "The Teahouse of the August Moon." Be set for something exotic, esoteric, recondite—and you'll have fun.

Incidentally, a Long Island reader, Mrs. Miriam Ruderfer, has written in to suggest that it may be intended as an allegory on modern Japan. The title, "Ugetsu," which means "the pale and mysterious moon after the rain," she thinks may be a reference to Japan after the war. The peasant who wants to be a samurai possibly "represents the Japanese Army that neglected the homeland to embark on a cockeyed dream of conquering the world." It is interesting, says Mrs. Ruderfer, that "his wife becomes a prostitute. Could be that Japan became a prostitute to the United States in the Japanese way of looking at our occupation?" And the peasant who dreams of riches, only to find that the dream is a ghost, seems to her to symbolize the folly of Japanese ambition for power.

Could be. We have no way of knowing what was in the producer's and director's minds. This inference of an allegory is as good as any that has occurred to us. And here again is a commentary on the comparative obscurity of Japanese films.

Motion Picture Herald
"J.R."

I t is rare indeed when a Japanese picture makes that long trip to these shores. "Rashomon" was the last one to be treated with critical acclaim and that was released more than two years ago. This latest import, "Ugetsu," is at least as good as its predecessor and in many respects superior. Its commercial appeal, of course, is limited to the art houses. Because of its generally slow-moving quality, its appeal becomes even more limited.

"Ugetsu" combines reality and fantasy, fact and legend, in a composite of cinematic beauty. It takes place in that period of Japanese history when feudal lords and their armies roamed the countryside terrorizing the villagers. It is the story of four of these peasants, their dreams, their emotions, their frailties.

One of the men is a potter whose greatest ambition is to sell his wares in the city. His wife merely wants the joys of a wife and mother. The other man is a farmer with ambitions of becoming a warrior with men at his command, to which his wife objects. When an army arrives at the village to begin looting, the four escape toward the city loaded with pottery. Because of the danger involved, the potter insists his wife and child return.

Once in the city they begin to make some money. The farmer takes his share and runs off to become a warrior, leaving his wife who eventually bears the shame of entering a brothel. The potter meets a wealthy and beautiful young girl under whose ghostly spell he falls. The tragedy which encompasses them all is delicately and touchingly portrayed.

Machiko Kyo and Masayuki Mori, both of whom starred in "Rashomon," play the wealthy girl and the potter. They, and the rest of the cast, all unknown, are remarkably adept at conveying emotions even to those whose knowledge of Japan, her people, and her history is remote.

The picture was produced by Masaichi Nagata and directed by Kenji Mizoguchi. The screenplay was adapted from the classic stories of Akinari Ueda. Special mention should be made of Kazuo Miyagawa's photography, much of which resembles fine painting. "Ugetsu" is a Daiei Film Production released here by Edward Harrison.

From *Motion Picture Herald* (18 September 1954): 145.

Time

F ive Japanese films have won grand prizes at International Film Festivals in Cannes and Venice since the war: *Rashomon* was the first to be shown in this country; *Ugetsu* is the second, and in many ways it is a jewel of intenser ray than *Rashomon*. *Rashomon* was orgiastic, almost Western in its rage for the things of the world. *Ugetsu* is contemplative in the midst of violence, wholly Oriental in its lidded introspection. As a result, its beauty and its meaning are more remote from Western audiences, but not too remote.

The story of *Ugetsu* comes from a Japanese classic, written in 1768 by Akinari Ueda. In the closing years of the 16th century, in a time of civil war, a country potter sees his chance to get rich quick selling pots in the city at war-inflated prices. The trip to the city, through a countryside full of marauding soldiery, is insanely dangerous. Halfway, the potter sends his wife and son back home alone. In town the pottery sells merrily, but no sooner is the money in hand than the potter begins to dream of luxury.

All at once the beautiful Lady Wakasa, attended by a dark old woman, appears, and asks him to bring some pottery to her house. He follows. She brings him tea; she offers him love. He cannot resist, "I never imagined such pleasures existed!" he cries. "You are my slave," she murmurs. At long last, a Buddhist priest frees the potter from her spell, and he turns back homeward. When he reaches home, he finds his wife dead. Only her spirit is there to comfort him, saying, "Go back to work."

Ugetsu is intended not as a story of real life, but as a fateful legend of the soul. Therefore, the actors keep closer than they did in *Rashomon* to the old symbolic style. If the greedy peasants grunt and draggle their arms like apes, it is not to say that the Japanese ever did so in real life, but rather that they assumed such attitudes in their hearts. In these terms, the painted mincing of the Lady Wakasa (Machiko Kyo, the rape victim in *Rashomon*), the snuffling animality of the potter (Masayuki Mori, the husband in *Rashomon*), the abstract dutifulness of the potter's wife satisfy the spectator as keenly as gestures in a well-made ballet.

The introverted mood of the picture is uncannily enhanced by the musical score. The cold, otherworldly picking of the *samisen* snips the threads of reality one by one, and the audience floats free among music that tries to express the intimate noises of the toiling spirit. The photography never once permits this mood to falter. Even the most violent scenes are dissolved in a meditative mist, like terrors in the mind of a sage. The moviegoer has the sense of living in a classic Japanese watercolor or of walking on a world that is really a giant pearl.

From *Time* (20 September 1954): 108.

Art
Eric Rohmer

T his week, a new masterpiece. I do not use this term lightly. If you have just seen *Ivan the Terrible,* run right over to see *Ugetsu.* As luck would have it, two of the "twelve best films of all time" (if you subscribe to the list recently published by the *Cahiers du Cinéma*) have come out in Paris almost simultaneously.

All of Paris should run to see this film. People who love the movies and people who don't care anything about them. Those who are interested in Japan and those who aren't. Like all great works, *Ugetsu* shatters the boundaries between genres and the frontiers between nations. There could be no better ambassador for Japanese civilization than this story drawn from medieval legends, subtitled so as to allow us to appreciate its extraordinary poetry. A world in appearance very different from ours will be revealed to you. You will perceive clearly the common source of our humanity, the crucible from which emerged both the *Odyssey* and the *Round Table* cycle, works with which *Ugetsu monogatari* has troubling analogies.

If you love Japanese films, go see this one. It's the most beautiful. If those that have been shown on our screens in the past have disappointed you, here is the opportunity to change your opinion. Kenji Mizoguchi, who died three years ago, was undoubtedly his country's greatest filmmaker. He was able to bend to his purpose an art form born in another part of the world, one whose potential his countrymen have not always been able to exploit fully. And yet you won't find in him any servile desire to copy the West. His conceptions of the frame, of acting, of rhythm, of composition, of time and space, are entirely homegrown. But he touches us in the same way Murnau, Ophuls, or Rossellini have touched us.

For the filmmaker as for the poet there is only one great subject: the idea of Unity hidden beneath the diversity of appearances or, translated into dramatic terms, if you prefer, the exalting and deceptive quest for a paradise where "all is luxury, calm, and pleasure."[1] And here this motif constitutes the very heart of the fable, since it shows us the mirages to which two peasants fall victim. One is tempted, like Don Quixote, by the demon of war; the other, like Lancelot, by the demon of the senses. But when this idea is translated into images, there is nothing abstract about it, and in this instance demonstrates the superiority of the Japanese filmmaker over the likes of us, products of the West, incapable of projecting the enchantment of fairy tales onto the screen. Our period films smack of masquerade; our fantastic films of trickery. This one doesn't.

---

1. A line from Baudelaire's poem, "L'Invitation au voyage" [translator's note].

From *Art,* no. 715 (25 March 1959): 5. Translated for this volume by Charles and Mirella Affron.

The elegant style of this film and the refinement of all its details hold infinitely rich lessons for us. But don't be alarmed. Seeing it is not like going to school. *Ugetsu* possesses, on top of everything else, a quality that you might have doubts about by reading my emphatic praise. The film is lively, engrossing, playful, easy, alternately moving and full of humor. It has nothing of the masterpiece's solemn, abstruse character. No hieratic quality, no Far Eastern slowness. On the contrary, you will be surprised, almost disappointed to see the words "The End" appear so quickly on the screen.

The Observer

Penelope Gilliatt

enji Mizoguchi, who died in 1956, was one of the greatest names in the whole astonishing Japanese cinema. No critic making lists of the world's best directors would leave him out; but on the other hand no one but a critic here has ever really had a chance to see his work. The airtight intellectual fame of being a neglected master must be one of the most bitter kinds of celebrity a film-maker can have.

Since the year of the General Strike, only one of his eighty-odd films has been shown publicly in England: it was a furiously eloquent piece about prostitution. (The people who handled it here, who would call Oedipus Rex "He desired his mother" if they had the chance, titled it "Street of Shame.") Now, at last, the Academy Cinema in its late-night shows is running "Ugetsu Monogatari," which is the film that the Japanese themselves think of as his masterpiece. It is set in the sixteenth-century epoch that was known as the "period of wars"; the title, which has hardly anything to do with it, opens out in English into "Tales of a Pale and Mysterious Moon after the Rain."

Mizoguchi's career began in the early twenties when the Japanese film industry was the most reactionary in the world, as well as the most chaotically inefficient; some of its admirers say that it still is. In the thirties, for instance, the men who spoke the commentaries to the silents fought a savage stalling action against the talkies. The fame and status of these living sub-titles often outshone the actors', and they looked on the sound-track as a shameful piece of automation. As militarism grew, the political censorship became more and more intense, and the moral censorship more and more absurd; it is only a few years since the watchdogs of Tokyo solemnly excised every kiss out of Western pictures.

Against this background of bigotry and hubbub, Mizoguchi remained unflustered and implacably critical. Eighty films in a working lifetime sounds like a man who pumps out American TV Westerns, but one comes nearer to Mizoguchi if one thinks of Chekhov. Technically, he makes Antonioni look like a man on crutches; he constructs his narratives in a series of concentrated, laconic scenes that expand in the head like the Oriental *haiku*, the verse form that Eisenstein called "a hieroglyph transposed into a phrase." His characters often express themselves as rudely as Chekhov's, with an accusing intimacy that breaks up the elaborate pattern of Japanese talk like a foot slipping during a quadrille.

Mizoguchi was trained as a painter, and his deep-focus shots often remind one of a Dutch interior. Even in the thirties he was using a perfectly ordinary sound-

From the London *Observer* (25 March 1962).

track to do all that directors with stereo might be doing now. "Ugetsu Monogatari" (1953) is filled with bursts of distant gunfire that seem to come out of one corner of the screen, and a rumpus that gathers over the dress circle from an approaching Japanese army, who in the movies always seem to creep up on the enemy with the noise of a squad of babies savaged by ducks.

Like many others before him, Mizoguchi's way of throwing sand in the censor's eyes was to dress a seditious story in period clothes.

The manner of some of his films is as wily as Brecht's and "Ugetsu Mono-gatari" is sometimes startlingly close to "Mother Courage." Like Brecht's epic, it begins with a wagon into which two brothers-in-law are loading their pottery. Sixteenth-century spivs, they have been running their eye over the landscape of the war like parasites choosing their host: one of them opts for the army, the other tries trade. The soldier, having become a hero by collaring the head of an enemy general who committed suicide and pretending that he lopped it off himself, goes downhill and visits a brothel where he finds his wife, who sarcastically demands to be paid for her services.

The merchant brother-in-law is taken up by an elegant princess who admires his pottery; little knowing that both she and her ravenously snobbish nurse are ghosts eager to marry into the real world, he wakes up one night with his supernatural Lady Ottoline Morrell and finds himself a bigamist. Eventually both men come home, chastened by death and privation, and find themselves more destitute than ever. The motives of war may be economic, says the film, but the last people to benefit from it are the poor.

Films and Filming
Paul Rotha

lmost unknown in Britain except for the memorable *Street of Shame,* the
work of the late Kenji Mizoguchi comes to us with an enviable reputation
from festivals and elsewhere. Going back to the silent days, he made more
than eighty films alternating between historical subjects and modern social problems, especially those related to women. In a recent international poll of critics in
Sight and Sound for the inevitable "ten best films of all time," *Ugetsu Monogatari*
achieved the remarkable distinction of coming into fourth place along with Stro-
heim's *Greed.* Frankly, I simply fail to understand why.

Made in 1953, three years before Mizoguchi's death, *Ugetsu*'s plot is based on
a collection of 18th-century stories by Akinari Ueda, famed for their blending of
realism and fantasy. The setting is 16th-century Japan—"the period of civil wars
and the Samuri"—when war comes to two families in a small village. The two
heads of family—a potter and a farmer—see in the war an opportunity to enrich
their lives. One wants material wealth, the other the glories of becoming a
Samurai. Together they set off: one leaves his wife behind but the other's wife
insists on accompanying the expedition. After many involved adventures both the
potter and the farmer partially succeed in their aims, but only at a cost to their
respective wives and to themselves. In the end they separately return to their
village to take up their old lives, wiser but poorer, but the potter finds only the
ghost of his wife to console him. This simple almost naive story is decked out with
a plethora of ghosts and orgies, mythical palaces and busy brothels.

I know that a lot of people will be talking about the poetic realism and the rich
visual sense with which Mizoguchi is supposed to have invested his film but then
so many Japanese films have these attributes. Especially those by Kurosawa,
whom I consider to be Mizoguchi's cinematic master in every way. It is said that
Mizoguchi liked to let his action develop in long shots. He certainly did and in
doing so becomes for me a pedestrian film-maker. There are, of course, some
isolated visually beautiful shots: what Japanese film hasn't. But overall I found the
direction turgid to the point of boredom and the acting on the level of good hokum.
I say the last with sadness because two of the cast, Machiko Kyo and Masayuki
Mori, were the husband and wife in *Rashomon* and gave such superlative performances under Kurosawa's direction.

The sub-titles—in American—must belong to some of the most banal which it
has been my fate to read. But let me add a brighter note—the music by Fumio
Hayasaka is strangely effective, quiet but restless, and makes a notable contribu-

From *Films and Filming* (May 1962): 30.

tion to a film which I found sadly undistinguished. When I read in the Press handout that "Mizoguchi has erected an epic structure of superb visual beauty and profound human insight" and "certain sequences shine out with a beauty one would not have thought possible in the cinema and which only a great graphic artist could have achieved," then I can only come to the conclusion that the writer and I must have been looking at different films.

Mizoguchi, we are told, was one of originators of the contemporary social problem film in Japan. If *The Street of Shame* was an example, then he indeed deserves our praise but I cannot extend it to period costume drama to which we are now submitted. Let us see some more of contemporary subject films and make a fresh assessment.

Commentaries

As the "Reviews" section has already indicated, *Ugetsu* quickly assumed the status of a masterpiece, so that within ten years of its release it was appearing on many critics' lists of the ten best films of all time. The "Commentaries" section presents a very small sampling of the critical study the film has received, but the variety of these essays testify to its complex fascination.

Several of the most frequently discussed qualities in Mizoguchi's work are taken up in this section. The sheer visual beauty of his films is considered in Joan Mellen's comments on the moral dimension of Mizoguchi's camera style and in Donald Richie's study of how such beauty leads the viewer to an awareness of broader symbolic meanings in the films. The director's particular interest in the role of women prompts Michel Mesnil's essay, and his rendering of the problematic relationship between reality and the dream draws the attention of Audie Bock and, in a more diffuse account, Felix Martialay. Bock praises Mizoguchi's ability to create "a cinematic assertion of the supernatural within the real," while Martialay emphasizes the self-reflexive aspect of *Ugetsu,* with Genjuro's dreaming echoing the creative dreaming of Mizoguchi himself.

Two critics help to place Mizoguchi within a Japanese context. Tadao Sato describes traditions in Japanese culture and religious belief that help to shape *Ugetsu,* while Robin Wood uses a contemporary, Ozu, to lead to a comprehensive account of the methods and assumptions of Mizoguchi's late films. The section begins with an essay by Alexandre Astruc, the French film director, who uses the achievements of Mizoguchi as the occasion for a meditation on the needs and concerns of the cinematic artist.

What Is Mise-en-Scène?

Alexandre Astruc

One need not have made many films to realize that *mise-en-scène* does not exist—that the actors perform very well by themselves, that any director of photography knows where to place his equipment to obtain a good frame, that the shots connect well by themselves, etc. Mizoguchi and Ophuls must have grasped this very quickly, and then passed on to what interested them. And what was that? To watch people move about? Not exactly. Rather to present them and at the same time to watch them act and be acted upon.

The difference between cinema and anything else, including the novel, is chiefly the impossibility of the camera to lie, and secondarily, the absolute certainty, shared by viewer and author alike, that on the screen everything will turn out well—in the long run. If the director intervenes anywhere in the production of a film, this is where he does so. He is caught between two premises: the image whereby he *captures* and the time whereby he *concludes*.

Concludes, not destroys: the slow erosion of truth which is the art of a Proust, its explosion as with a Faulkner, presuppose that the novel is written with words, fragments of eternity. It defines reality, it is at the cost of a constant effort of decomposition, of a destruction of forms, of a forward movement thrown against the attack of a vocabulary, of which the flow carries the debris away.

The camera defines; it does not surpass, it observes reality. It is naive to believe that the systematic use of a wide-angle lens can change the course of events. To compensate for this passivity, the camera does not lie. What the lens captures is the movement of the body, revealing immediately *as is* everything physical—the dance, a woman's glance, a change of gait, beauty, truth, etc.

Cinema presumes a certain trust in the world as it is. Even in the midst of ugliness, even in the midst of misery: in fact, it is here where it uncovers that strange and cruel tenderness, the dread sweetness of *Hiroshima,* where, after evoking so many horrors, a few quick traveling sequences in the center of a city and a woman's voice are sufficient to throw the whole landscape into human perspective, as if, quite naturally and through some strange device, all its latent hope should one day be fulfilled. . .

One of the most beautiful films ever made was done by an old Japanese director—author of nearly a hundred films—with undoubtedly no other desire than the honest exercise of his profession. After five minutes of projection, *Ugetsu* shows clearly what direction is—at least for some. It is a certain way of extending

From *Cahiers du Cinema in English,* no. 1 (January 1966): 53–55. Originally published in *Cahiers du Cinéma,* no. 100 (October 1959): 13–16.

the *élans* of the soul into the movements of the body. It is a song, a rhythm, a dance. Mizoguchi knows well that what is expressed in physical violence is something which cannot be falsified. Not character, not self-comprehension, but that irresistible forward movement which always springs out along the same paths in pursuit of fulfillment—or destruction. I rather imagine that what interests him after so many films is no longer the spectacle, but the fact of not being able to turn one's eyes away from the spectacle. An author writes perhaps to deliver himself, a director also does so but never entirely. In the tenderness or horror of the universe he exploits, he will have to hit upon what, strictly speaking, one could call a certain forwardness or helpful complicity, but what for the artist is never more than the source of the grandeur that obsesses and what he believes he can reveal.

What, then, becomes of technique? It ceases to be a method of displaying—or concealing. Style is not a certain way of rendering the ugly beautiful and vice versa. No director in the world will have confidence in photography alone if his ambition is not limited to competing with Yvon. It is even more than interpretation; traveling sequences are not notes or explanatory references at the bottom of a page. It seems to me that it has no other goal than to create that mysterious distance between the author and his characters, whose stylized movements seem to accompany so faithfully the oscillations and mad courses through the forest.

But this only *seems* to be so, for the power and grandeur of this universe which again and again in work comes from the author's constant domination of its elements. He bends these elements, perhaps not to his own vision—Mizoguchi is a director, not a novelist—but to satisfy his need to see them at a distance, which is wisdom or the desire for wisdom. Thus the tragic poem has its force in the apparent insensitivity and coldness of the artist who seems installed, camera in hand, at the bend in the river, surveying the plain where the actors of the drama are to emerge.

The exquisite and touching delicacy of *Ugetsu* is made, as in certain Westerns, of that irremediable slowness which, if only by violence and anger, drives on a handful of individuals whose destinies are insignificant.

But Mizoguchi knows well that, after all, it is not very important for his film to turn out well; he is more concerned with knowing whether the strongest bonds between himself and his characters are those of tenderness or contempt. He is like the viewer who seeks the reflection of pleasure on the features of the one he watches, even though he also knows quite well that it is not this reflection alone which he is seeking but perhaps quite simply the tedious confirmation of something he has always known but cannot refrain from verifying.

So I consider *mise-en-scène* as a means of transforming the world into a spectacle given primarily to oneself—yet what artist does not know instinctively that what is seen is less important than the way of seeing, or a certain way of *needing to see* or be seen.

Between the canvas and the shapes which haunt him, what the painter introduces is not a different way of observing, but a new dimension. A picture by Manet is not "nature seen through a temperament" but a landscape through which an esthetic will has passed, irreducible to themes as well as to the secret motivations of the artist, upon which it may nourish itself, but which will never wear it out. Direction is not exclusively the will to give a new sense to the world, but nine times out of ten it is organized around the secret certainty of withholding a piece of truth about man first, about the work of art afterwards. These are indissolubly bound together. Mizoguchi avails himself of violence, greed, or sexual desire to express on the screen what he cannot release unless these elements are encountered. But it would be absurd to say that violence is the subject of his films; if he needs it, it is like an alcoholic needs drink—to feed his intoxication, not to fulfill it. With Mizoguchi, as with all the great masters of the screen, it is never the plot that comes to the fore, nor the form, nor even the effect, nor again the possibility of bringing frantic characters face to face in extreme situations. Mizoguchi, like most Orientals, laughs at psychology and verisimilitude. He needs violence as a lever—to seesaw into another universe. But as a baroque painting, the storm-rains which fall on those grimacing faces and dismantled bodies presage the abatement. Beyond desire and violence, the world of the Japanese, like that of Murnau, draws the veil of indifference where, in an "exotic" cinema, the metaphysical suddenly intrudes.

Is there, after all, much of a difference between a Japanese director conversant enough with his profession to be offered a seven-year Hollywood contract (which closely resembles the hiring of an engineer "by the month") and a "maudit" poet in the style of the end of the 19th Century? Baudelaire's opium and Mizoguchi's profession really have the same function: they are pretexts, like Proust's asthma or homosexuality, like the yellow on which Van Gogh would become intoxicated. But who can say that the yellow has always been the subject of Van Gogh's paintings and not his goal? The artist searches where he believes he can find the conditions for his creation; the director at the studio, at the brothel, or at the museum. . . .

The universe of an artist is not the one that dominates him, but the one he needs to create, and to transform it perpetually into something which obsesses him still more than that by which he is obsessed.

The obsession of the artist is artistic creation.

Distance and Beauty in the Films of Mizoguchi
Donald Richie

Mizoguchi, unlike many film directors, was consistently interested in mythic situations, in symbolic configurations that implied more than they actually showed. When one sees *Sansho Dayu,* for example, one is seeing much more than a picture about a tyrant and a distraught mother—one is seeing *the* suffering woman. To see *The Life of Oharu* is to see much more than a simple chronicle of a fall of a woman; one sees *the* fall and the woman becomes archetypal. In *A Tale from Chikamatsu,* the unfortunate lovers become *the* lovers, just as Romeo and Juliet become *the* lovers. Mizoguchi's true interest is always in what his situation and his characterization implies; he always suggests that both mean more than merely human adventures happening to particular humans. He insists upon the universal, the general—and at times, as in *Ugetsu,* his interest becomes nearly allegorical.

Insofar as any filmmaker is free to express his personal vision (and Mizoguchi, being a professional filmmaker working for a commercial company, made many pictures which do not appear to be mythic), Mizoguchi was consistent to this salient fact of his style. In *Foggy Harbor* (1923) the heroine (suggested by O'Neill's Anna Christie) remains mysterious because she is not only herself but also a symbol for the unknown, for adventure; in *The Sisters of the Gion* (1936) the two sisters are not only real people in their own right, they are also the Old versus the New. Even in such a standard program picture as *Musashi Miyamoto* (1945), the hero is shown as a real person but the content is such that he is also heroism personified.

The context of the Mizoguchi film prepares and makes possible this feeling of things larger than they appear to be, this symbolism and allegory. In many of his later films, the context is that of the fairy tale or myth. *Sansho Dayu* begins with shots of ruined pillars, the time-eroded remnants of the slave-camp palace—the story we are about to see has long finished, it is history, it is fairy tale. We watch the adventures of mother and children with the detachment we give myth, and Mizoguchi, by insisting on sheer visual beauty, makes us understand that we are watching a romantic adventure rather than a real-life story. There is that famous scene where mother, children, nurse wander through the field of flowering rushes. The camera stays far away (it is through the long shot that Mizoguchi achieved this feeling of distance so necessary to his purpose) and we think of tales of adventures, of other lost mothers/lost children stories we know, we think of the

The original English version has been lost. This article has been retranslated, with the author's approval, from the Japanese translation, which appeared in *Kino* (February 1965).

archetypal situation of mother and children lost and nowhere to go, one of the strains of myths of any country.

In *Ugetsu* we are truly in fairy-tale country, where the dead are raised, the future is accurately foretold, and ghosts appear. In *Yokihi* again the dead appear—those disembodied voices at the end of the picture—and we recognize great mythic patterns in the simple potter who finds and loses love, in the great emperor and his queen who lose all through love.

Mizoguchi creates this context through distance. There is the distance of camera to subject; then there is the distance in time; and, most important, there is the distance that can only be achieved by engaging yet alienating our emotions by telling us something we already know. When this is prepared, Mizoguchi (who studied to be a painter and remained an amateur painter throughout his life) makes use of one of the great and unacknowledged distance-makers of his medium—pictorial beauty.

The effect of beauty in the cinema has never been properly evaluated. The camera is known for its ability to reproduce actuality, for its inability not to. We have become so accustomed to this function that we usually no more think of doubting the camera than we would of doubting our own eyes. Supernal beauty on the screen has therefore the same value that supernal beauty has in life: we are hushed, we are taken aback, and we are moved. At the same time, we realize that in film we are looking at a picture. This realization is a sudden one because until then we had been believing in the actuality we are being shown. At this instant we then must consider not only the scene but also the hand of the artist.

For example, we are looking at *Ugetsu,* already caught in its story. The lady has come to the outdoor pool and has removed her clothing. She and the potter are in the water and the camera glides away in a slow pan. This is discreet, we may think; then we see that the camera is following the path of the water; this is logical, we may think; then the camera pans upward and there is a magnificent lawn with a lake shimmering in the distance and the lovers are on a distant square of matting, their position absolutely balanced by a single tree, a perfect composition of the most radiant and gratuitous beauty. And what do we think then?—Nothing. We can only think of Mizoguchi.

When this occurs in a film the common critical complaint is that the camera has called attention to itself, that the director is being arty. This is true, but it is nothing to complain of since it is through devices such as these that the director achieves the final distance—a distance achieved through a beauty so great that our belief disappears. We cannot see the characters as people, cannot (literally) believe in them after having been surprised by gratuitous beauty in this fashion. Mizoguchi's aim is achieved. We must see the characters as something more meaningful—we must seem them as symbols.

Mizoguchi films are a fascinating experience because we must see them—most of his later films—on this double level. We feel deeply for the mother in *Sansho Dayu* as a much persecuted human being and yet, at the same time, since we know we are seeing a fairy tale, since we are always surprised by scenes of beauty, we come to realize that the film is not only about this human being—it is about what this human being symbolizes, it is about us, as all fairy tales are about us.

The psychological implications of, say, *Ugetsu* are clear enough: it is an allegory of the soul; those of *Sansho Dayu*, of *Oharu*, of *Yokihi* are different, but similar, and it is these implications which both conceal and reveal the richness of the Mizoguchi film. One might compare him with other directors. In a way the nearest parallel is Marcel Carné who, whenever he could, made pictures about love betrayed; a parallel less close is the young John Huston who used to make pictures about great quests which came to nothing, his implications being that the quest (in which *African Queen, The Treasure of Sierra Madre, The Maltese Falcon*—even *Moby Dick*) was everything, the result nothing.

Mizoguchi's implication is that the world is as it is, and our lot is to endure it, to live with and through it, and that if this is not pleasing (and I cannot think of a major Mizoguchi film with a 'happy' ending) it at least lets us know that we are living. His heroines (for he has naturally found women, particularly in Japan, closer to his truth than the men) all discover this fact and either die content despite all (as in *Sansho,* in *Oharu,* in *Chikamatsu,* in *Yokihi*) or, seeing this, decide to continue a bit longer with the game (as in *Akasen Chitai,* also called *Street of Shame, Gionbayashi,* and *Woman of the Night*). Is it this mythology, I wonder, which accounts for his contemporary appeal—now, seven years after the director's death?

He is the only Japanese director whom the French have taken to their hearts; the Germans have detected something they understand very well in his films; even the English are more attracted to him than to any other Japanese director. And the example of America—where the films of Mizoguchi are, except for *Ugetsu,* unknown and where others (*Oharu, Sansho Dayo*) have been misunderstood. It is as though this acquiescence to the world as it is, this emphasis upon existence as the only end, is a message grateful to Europe and not, as yet, to America.

To one living in Japan the wisdom of Mizoguchi is seen at once, because this is the wisdom of traditional Japan, and the Japanese are quite right to see Mizoguchi as one of their most typical and traditional filmmakers. Like all his contemporaries he believed in distance, he revered the past, and he sought wisdom in acquiescing to the world as it (unfortunately or not) happened to be. This he has shown in all of his major pictures—and has added that one element that is salient to traditional Japanese art: beauty is the means through which this inner wisdom is at last achieved.

The Master Mizoguchi in Six Critical Perspectives: *Ugetsu*
Felix Martialay

I have to warn that I have not seen the film more than twice. The first time was two or three years ago. I didn't take any notes at that time. That first occasion only allowed me to view the film the second time with a greater serenity; to be at ease concerning the intricacies in the subject matter, which in itself is something. For the second viewing, I was all set with sheets of paper and a ballpoint pen, but I never used them. The fascination of the film was so complete, so all-absorbing, that by the end of the showing I had written nothing more than the title.

If the above words seem to explain the evanescent quality of what I will now write, I want to remove myself even further from the whole gamut of topics concerning the Oriental film, in order to carry out this task free of that baggage. Stereotypes, occult Japanese symbols, an incomprehension of that country's customs—none of these are pertinent here. *Ugetsu* seems to me to be a very hermetic, very ambiguous, very complicated film, but not because of its Oriental source but for the perfection of its workmanship, for the sheer height of its artistic quality. This is its greatest difficulty. The superior artistry of Mizoguchi requires a preparation and an effort on the part of the spectator that doesn't always begin—I don't always begin—to capture all its poetry and grandeur.

For the critic, it would be very convenient to seize on these Oriental exoticisms in order to fill the vacuum that is due above all to the critic's lack of artistic acumen, rather than to localisms. *Ugetsu* is, above all, cinema. Total cinema. Cinema of here and there, independent of any specific place. If the film seems hermetic, it is not due to its geographic location but rather to its artistic richness. Good proof of that is that in *Ugetsu* one finds Anthony Mann, Rossellini, Renoir, Murnau, Dreyer, Bergman, Welles, Preminger, Nicholas Ray . . . there are traits and details of all the great creative masters in this film because, in the richness of its status as a masterpiece, it has to have strong affinities in terms of forms of appearances with the moments inspired by these directors, no matter what their nationality.

At the outset, *Ugetsu* is a work that is "larger than life," larger than Mizoguchi himself. It is, in reality, the life of Mizoguchi, his quintessence, his death. The work of a chosen one whom God has permitted to see his dream realized. (Mizoguchi is the potter Genjuro. The dialogue of Genjuro with Princess Wakasa is a treatise of aesthetics and, at the same time, of ethics. The film-princess is the temptation that kills but saves, something like the palm of the martyr that dies and saves, but one must accept this death in order to reach salvation.)

From *Film Ideal* (15 January 1965): 44–45. Translated by Linda C. Ehrlich and David G. Anderson for this volume.

In order to understand *Ugetsu*, it is necessary to have an extraordinary mastery over the material, and an extraordinary mastery over one's own human nature in order to give free rein to the mastery of the artist over his art.

This is possibly the first great theme of the film, the theme of the artist, of art. To give evidence of one's time is to give it of oneself as an individual immersed in that time. But evidence is secondary to the artist; it is something extra, because the main thing is to produce beauty. This beauty will be its own unique justification. But this beauty is the result of those tensions, that have solicited it, that have pushed it. Of these tensions, that of its own presence in this time is certainly not the most minor one. The problem of *Ugetsu*, the conscious problem, is that of Mizoguchi himself, an artist who wants to know the value of his "clay" and who dreams of beauty only to awaken, turning his potter's wheel, making film after film with the simplicity of an artisan who has no illusions about anything. *Ugetsu* is, actually, the Princess Wakasa of Mizoguchi, that creature of luxury that is a fantasy, madness, fascination, fire. . . . All of this has possessed him completely, bringing into existence the beautiful dream that is this film. Afterwards, until death separated him from his camera, the potter continued; the dream had passed. *Ugetsu* had arisen from his intellect and his heart.

Mizoguchi forcefully expresses in this film the madness of the creator—in that fire that possesses Genjuro, that makes him ignore the danger of the unchained hordes, his sobbing family, in order to keep up the oven where his works were being fired. It is that alienation that makes him forget what and who he is, what he has left behind, everything, in order to submerge himself in the ecstasy of beauty.

This causes us, in the first place, to philosophize with the author about reality and fiction, the real and the fantastic, what is lived and what is dreamed; about the pleasure of hours yet to come, about feelings and the illusion of those feelings, about real beings and guiding or destructive "phantasmas."

There are no boundaries between dream and reality. Or, if there is one, it is as ambiguous as those political boundaries which no accident of geographical relief explains.

Hence, in *Ugetsu*, let us not distinguish dream, hallucination, memory, or the mental image, from reality. We live reality with the protagonist in the same form that we dream our nightmare without knowing that it, indeed, is a nightmare; without distinguishing it from our conscious world. But, in the end—what difference is there between sleep and waking? None, in the moment of dreaming. Although we know perfectly well that only our waking hours have a physical reality and that dreams don't exist, this doesn't impede us from seeing and living both ways. All that we dream is the truth that we are dreaming, and it is the truth while we dream it. The truth that we dream and the truth that we live are the same. Then permit me the same sophism as Mizoguchi when he arrives at the conclusion that to deny the dreamt truth would be to deny the living truth. And that would be to deny everything.

For that reason Mizoguchi doesn't establish differences or distances. There isn't any conceit or "flow" or evocative music. Everything is realism. A violent realism mixed with the most outrageous lyricism, the living with the dead, real beings with fantastic ones, the unreal world with the real.

Because enormous foundations are needed in order to raise skyscrapers to the sky, it is also necessary to take root totally in reality, in order to elevate one's fantasies. Images that are always realistic, always in the present.

Even though it may later turn out that the artist is the only one who dreams an ideal separate from reality. The potter does not idealize a reality—except when he thinks of his wife in the kimono stall—rather he begins an ideal world with an ideal woman, an ideal palace, an ideal love.

Even so, in short, it is not important whether one dreams or not, because every film is a dream, and the fact that inside this dream there is another is not important. If we accept the first dream, why not accept the second that is integrated in it?

It is possible that other critics will see in the film—more than a testimonial to that dream of the creator and to the anguish this creation produces for him—a work with various "theses." Each one will favor a different one of these, because it is certain that each person sees in a film of this caliber what he wants to see, what he desires that it show him. I am inclined toward the Mizoguchian ambiguity. In that ambiguity the following ideas stand out, each given the same weight:

- war as the source of all calamity (Tobei says: "War has torn the spirit");
- ambition as the destroyer of the most solid human principles (as Tobei also says, "Ambition must be like the ocean, without limits");
- fatalism as an expression of the fight between the sky and the earth, between the gods and humans (beings dragged over the earth, stooped over, always on their knees as if flattened by a superior force that impedes their standing erect, their domination; spirits in constant defiance, desirous of standing proud, of dominating);
- a negation of all adventure, of all spiritual and social rebellion;
- an affirmation of conformity, in a system of social classes, in a lack of communication;
- an apology for destruction. All of the characters have an itinerary that leads them to their self-destruction. While Tobei buys a dazzling breastplate with which to begin the path of "samurai," Ohama, his wife, is raped and paid off (a reiteration of images of the purse of the false "samurai" paying for his illusion, and of the group of soldiers giving their salary to the violated woman). While Genjuro the potter falls drunk with wine and lust onto the picnic cloth in the garden after his bath, Miyagi, his wife, falls "doubly" dead. "My fall is the price of your ascension," says Ohama. In contrast, Tobei's fall occurs when he finds his own wife in a brothel.
- a hymn of devotion to women. It is not a question of repeating what Julio Martínez wrote in the article "Words and Words, No Images to Draw Us Closer to Mizoguchi," published on page 7 of the previous issue of *Film Ideal*, 159, pointing to this attribute. The women in *Ugetsu* conserve their

lucidity; even more, they possess a greater lucidity than the men; they know what they are going to suffer because of the men; they see almost simultaneously into the present and the future; they know their destiny and they fulfill it with their sacrifice. The lucidity extends to Princess Wakasa who already knows her illusory being and the outcome of her forcefully expressed love, even at the time that she gives the offering to the potter. The men, on the other hand, are blind to their destiny. They swagger with passion, neither weighing its overflowing force nor foreseeing its scope.

In my opinion, the ambiguity originates in the fact that Mizoguchi doesn't resolve anything in his film. And, at the same time, he resolves everything for us: both what I have said and what I have not even looked at carefully here. He doesn't resolve things because he is limited to showing the beauty of a simple world, whose existence would not be possible without the dream, without the illusion, without desire. The Mizoguchian man needs his own experience, not an inherited one, not one told to him. A lived experience, even if living it out costs him his very life. Man, and even more if he is an artist, needs to be fascinated by fascination, to dream the dream, to be endangered by danger, and to die in life. Only in this way can he return, as did Tobei and Genjuro, and appreciate the beauty of daily life, of the ordinary, of peace, of life.

This is what conditions the repetition of identical scenes whose difference lies in their shading. When a man walks, he walks. If we shade the direction, we know if he is going or returning. If we include him in the landscape, we give the direction and its consequence—going or returning—but the act is the same: to walk. From this double itinerary, of the venturing out to, and return from, the dream, from experience, from life, from illusion, there are repeated points although they are geometrically symmetrical. In Mizoguchi, the geometry is the drama. (In Fritz Lang, drama was the geometry; in Cottafavi, the geometry is the appearance of the drama.) Mizoguchi's moral posture is the contemplation of that double itinerary: an indolent, distanced contemplation, an indifferent contemplation. A total objectivization.

The slowness of Mizoguchi. This is the grand myth. And in this respect I remember the novels of Karl May in the Winnetu series; the novelist spoke of the cursed horses—some of exceptionally pure blood that had a speed that was quite superior to that of a normal horse, but, even more, had the trait that when a magical word was whispered to them, they took on additional speed that made them run like the wind. Well then, Mizoguchi is a "cursed" director. his films have an oppressive tempo; a very rapid pace, but when one thinks they are going at top speed, the story takes on even a greater speed that leaves the spectator exhausted. *Ugetsu* is a veritable shower of emotional and highly expressive blows, each impelled by the other.

The conciseness in the story makes each shot, each frame, pregnant with meaning modified in each expression, in each movement, of his actors. (Mizoguchi's cinema is one of mobile lines: his actors.) All of it turns and turns like a maddened carousel that leaves breathless anyone intent on following it in detail. Everything runs, moves, and is moved about with an astonishing velocity, even when the camera is practically still. (It is still, for example, in the death of Miyagi and, nevertheless, what the camera sees is truly dizzying: the flight of the woman with the child, the rice, the soldiers who pursue them, the encounter, the struggle, the first fall, the child, the rice, the second fall, the agony, the soldiers distributing the stolen rice among themselves, death, the soldiers eating. . . . What a marvel! Three simultaneous actions. And the camera is still, astonished, exhausted from having filtered and filtered movements, passions, passages, life, death. . . .)

The speed that is in the music, ringing like the hooves of galloping horses over a rock, in the dialogue, throwing out the words violently, in the movements of the characters who are almost epileptic and febrile. . . . Speed in the laconic, in the nakedness, in the correctness. . . . It is the fire of the creator in a "state of grace" that is reflected in these spasms prolonged by the madness of not losing the dream, of not allowing to escape that magical alienation that consumes him in privileged instants of which he has to take full advantage.

The same could be said in many scenes: the declaration of the princess—what an impressive ballet, with her revolving around him with her erect figure while Genjuro retreats, turns, drags himself, bending himself double at the sight of the maid who is actually directing the dance, cornering the couple more and more— the bath, the picnic in the country, the invasion of the soldiers, the rupture between the potter and Wakasa, the awakening of the artist. Each contemplated situation has, in its repetition, a meaning which is deeper, more complete, more total.

The *mise-en-scène*—here is the true difficulty with Mizoguchi. It is difficult because of its uncommon richness that one has to capture—very slowly, in all of its nuances. I suppose that to see *Ugetsu* in the hand-viewer (for editing) has to be something really beautiful and worthy of study by someone who wants to direct and not make himself look ridiculous. (Mizoguchi has taken to such a high level the job of film directing that it would be difficult for him to contain his laughter on seeing what is concretely understood these days as a cinematic work.) A really audacious *mise-en-scène* that enters, without any detour, in the interior life of the characters, with an astonishing sobriety in spite of the apparent baroque style of the multicolored images, full, brimming with strong points, with actions and meanings. With a simple movement of the body contemplated in all its distance traveled, we are given insight into the faintest trembling of a soul.

Normally he works in long shots, sequential shots in medium or general frame. There are very few close-up shots—the one of Princess Wakasa in the market is an exception and, for this reason, it has an unforgettable impact—and almost total abolition of the countershot. It is, then, the totality of the bodies—human or objects—that express everything. The body in movement, vibrating, stopped, but without ever being isolated from its milieu (forests, water, rooms, streets, air . . .) but rather living in it and with it. Land, rain, flowers, forests (Bergman), lakes.

(What perfect integration of life and death, beings and things, material and atmosphere, in the scene of the parting of the husband and wife on the lake, and the meeting in the mist with the boat carrying the dying man.)

The camera does not create the *mise-en-scène* but captures it whole, although in order to do so it has to fly up to incredible heights, or to drag itself through water or along the floor; it also goes where an emotional tension is produced between beings or objects, capturing that tension and its consequences.

Mizoguchi Kenji
Michel Mesnil

T he greatest originality of the *Tales* is precisely to be found in its painting of conjugal love. Mizoguchi makes of this love an idea that does not fit within a bourgeois framework. The atmosphere of tender love and of whispered complaisance that reigns between Genjuro and Miyagi brings the sound of attained passion—a sound new to the cinema—to a delicate equilibrium, one that is always menaced since the potter will betray his love for a beautiful and risky adventure and, returning home, will meet up with a deferred punishment. The return to the home—which is certainly one of the most beautiful scenes ever filmed, because it is one of the fullest, the most charged with interior life, as in a painting by Chardin—is for Genjuro the explosion of happiness, although it turns out to be an illusory happiness: Mizoguchi is more cruel than Max Ophuls— felicity regained after the agonizing wound and perpetual incompleteness of pleasure and peril. In regaining his home space, the man suddenly finds himself no longer in agreement with others and with society. In fact, his house isolates him more from the outside world than could the palace of a snake-woman, a sojourn that was uncomfortable since dangers and memory beat their way in from all sides. In contrast, in the single room of his wooden house, he feels perfectly at ease, protected from all peril. This pilgrimage back to origins is like a reunion with the warmth of the maternal breast, an asylum where, Mizoguchi seems to suggest, active and adventurous spirits may dream of more than other people do. Stretched out on a ordinary futon, in a corner of the room, he falls sleep quickly, mumbling about his well-being while his wife calmly devotes herself to some needlework and while a weak light watches over, like life itself, the heart of this closed world. In the morning, just as the cold of the early hours will penetrate, through the broken joints of the devastated house, into the soul of Genjuro to disillusion him, so will the hard truth of the world strike him in the face.

The opposition between Miyagi and Wakasa is thus not at all between a tranquil love fully open to the world of others and an exclusive passion, or between conjugal affection, as one conventionally speaks of it, and wild love [*l'amour fou*]. Between Wakasa and Miyagi, it is the latter who offers the true image of passion— a passion lived to the limits of a Calvary and death—and it is the latter who, better than the former, open to all compromises, maintains the hero in the full bliss of his solitude. To a certain degree, in fact, the impassioned Miyagi must be carrying insider her a Wakasa that the troubles of life have suffocated. The two women are

From *Mizoguchi Kenji* by Michel Mesnil (Paris: Editions Seghers, 1965), pp. 75–77. Translated by Dana Polan for this volume.

undoubtedly opposed at the level of the man's attitude as fidelity versus betrayal. Yet in fact, eroticism and love have the same goal, but the latter is simply stronger than the former: both want to be free of social constraints and it is for that reason that they are in opposition. Miyagi and Wakasa, each in her own way, offer Genjuro havens of interior peace where he can restore himself far from the "vile multitudes." They weave cocoons around the man that isolate him from others. A love that separates, forever.

Let us offer a counterproof of the truth of this interpretation. The fate of beings without love—who are always women, and toward whom Mizoguchi is not lacking in a degree of sadism—is to fall victim, sooner or later, to a society that ignores them, that despises them, as it does all living beings. Like those monsters imagined by H. G. Wells who, coming from Mars, could not arm themselves against the attack of invisible enemies against which they were impotent, deprived of their natural environment, Oharu and Madame Yuki were not able to create around themselves, whether because of bad luck or misery, the impenetrable web of love which alone can offer to the living being its first haven of sweet warmth. These figures will mercilessly be delivered over to the Other like the thief thrown to the dogs. One sees what the social entity does with them: suicide, exploitation, and death—this is their lot. It is also the lot of Yang-Kwei-Feï, of the boarders in *Street of Shame:* deprived of the only "others" that count, those by whom one is loved, they succumb or disappear.

To be sure, Mizoguchi's conception of love does not at all counter what we can term his humanism. The exaltation of the couple to the detriment of society, of love as the power of separation, the triumph of the individual solitude (when he does in fact triumph)—this aristocratic attitude or this unconscious anarchism do not stop Mizoguchi from indicating to Yoda: "Miyagi must give the impression that in her native village there is the tomb of her parents, fields that are passed down from century to century, the changing of the seasons each year, people who live on the land and will be buried in that very same land." One sees from this how Genjuro the vagabond—every man who falls from the nest is a vagabond until a new love stabilizes him—recovers, by finding his wife, the entire community of men. But this recovery does not come from a brutal insertion into the group nor from a direct feeling of camaraderie or fraternity. Human he certainly is, and he is from a land and a village, but what interests Mizoguchi about him is the individual and not the collective. Genjuro can feel collective and rooted only through the rootedness and the lineage of Miyagi who is more naturally social than he since she is a woman. Their union makes them, by this indirect path, into members of a larger family, the great house of humankind. But they only know this in rare and muffled moments since for the most part they live for themselves, for the solitude of the couple, for the love that connects them to each other and cuts them off from the rest.

Mizoguchi: The Ghost Princess and the Seaweed Gatherer
Robin Wood

An attempt to define the art of Mizoguchi can usefully take as its starting point comparison with his great contemporary Ozu. I must say at once that any definition must be tentative in the extreme, being based on only a small proportion of each director's work: I've seen about a dozen Mizoguchis and only half as many Ozus, mainly late works in both cases. The enterprise is further complicated by the great range of subject matter and expression within Mizoguchi's work. Rather than attempt to offer generalizations that would cover even all his accessible films, I am limiting this article to only two, though they seem to me the greatest and most completely representative of those I have seen: *Sansho Dayu* (*Sansho the Bailiff*) and *Ugetsu Monogatari*. They are closely related to each other, and the other late works—including those with a modern setting like the magnificent *Uwasa No Onna* (*Woman of Rumor*) and even a film as different in obvious ways as *Street of Shame*—can be seen to relate significantly to them: one might reasonably claim that they represent, together, a central core within Mizoguchi's late period, though others might wish to make similar claims for *Shin Heike Monogatari* or *Yang Kwei Fei*.

Although Ozu and Mizoguchi, when juxtaposed, appear in many ways polar opposites, both have been placed in opposition to the more western- (and "western"-) influenced Kurosawa. Kurosawa's work is studded with adaptations of western literature; his films not only show the influence of the western cinema but lend themselves in turn to adaptation, so that at least four have been re-made in Hollywood or Italy. No one seems to be rushing to re-make *Tokyo Story* or *Sansho* in an American setting, though the subject matter of neither would present insuperable difficulties. The films' tone and style are felt as somehow indigenously Japanese, though it is difficult to link them beyond a somewhat loose application of the adjective "contemplative." Mizoguchi's style shows greater affinities with that of Ophuls on the one hand and Rossellini on the other than with that of any other Japanese director within my experience, yet one doesn't think of him as in any sense deriving from European cinema: any resemblances seem fortuitous, a matter of spiritual affinity rather than influence in either direction. One guesses that the late styles of both Mizoguchi and Ozu are the product of a long period of evolution within the Japanese cinema, and, beyond it, within Japanese culture.

Ozu's visual compositions are dominated by the square and the rectangle: Mizoguchi's are characterized by an equally striking and pervasive emphasis on diagonals. The tendency of Ozu's cinema is towards a series of "stills." His

From *Film Comment* 9, no. 2 (March-April 1973): 32–40.

characters either face the camera directly or sit or stand at right angles to it. The square or rectangular patterns of the decor—walls or doorways or windows—often frame them as if to enclose each in his or her separate compartment. Each image takes on the quality of a framed picture, as if cut off from any outer world beyond the confines of the screen. Characters almost never enter or leave the frame during a shot: the unity and enclosedness of the image is rigorously preserved. The spectator's eye is directed always towards the figure at the center of the composition, almost never towards the periphery.

The composition even of static dialogue scenes in Mizoguchi is habitually built on diagonals cutting across the screen. The actors are placed at oblique angles to the camera, and so are the mats on which they sit; where Ozu tends to place his actors squarely against walls or doorways, Mizoguchi typically uses a corner as focal point. However beautifully organized the composition (and there are no more beautiful compositions anywhere in the cinema), the diagonals invariably lead the eye outwards, always implying a world beyond the frame. What is true of interiors is equally so of exteriors. Paths cross the screen diagonally: in *Ugetsu* the boat bearing the dying fisherman emerges through the mist at an oblique angle to the boat poled by Ohama; in *Madame Yuki* a speedboat and its wake cut a diagonal line across the image.

This contrast is reinforced by the totally opposed camera styles of the two directors. In late Ozu the camera virtually never moves: to cut from static image to static image is to detach and separate little segments of the world as objects of contemplation. In late Mizoguchi the camera moves in the great majority of shots, and the movements are frequently long and elaborate; to move the camera so that one part of the world is excluded while another is framed, is to unite, to make connections. If "Cinema of Contemplation" is a phrase applicable to the work of both directors, it is a much more adequate description of Ozu than of Mizoguchi: the contemplative aspect of the latter's work is continually balanced, and at times superseded, by its dynamism. And a general observation about the content of their respective *oeuvres* is relevant here. Both deal recurrently with the theme of the Family; but where characteristically Ozu's people are finally separate, alone, Mizoguchi's move almost invariably towards union, mystical rather than physical, even when some of them are dead. The stylistic differences are clearly related to—if not actually expressive of—this opposition in overall movement.

An example will help to clarify the part played by the contemplative in Mizoguchi's style. Consider (as representative rather than exception) the brief scene in *Sansho* where Zushio, seeking redress for the horrors Sansho has perpetrated, attempts to confront the minister with a petition and is overcome and dragged away to prison by guards. The tracking-shot that accompanies Zushio's desperate efforts to be heard is far from contemplative: it involves the viewer very directly in the scene's hectic movement, in the urgency and near-hysteria of the young man. Mizoguchi doesn't cut away to show us the guards approaching—they suddenly erupt into the frame from all sides. This is immediately recognizable as a recurrent motif in Mizoguchi's films:

other striking examples are the mother's attempted escape from the island of Sado in *Sansho* and the rape of Ohama in *Ugetsu*. The sudden intrusion of hostile, menacing forces into the foreground of the image, surrounding and overwhelming the protagonist, forcefully expresses the director's sense of the precariousness of things, the continual imminence of disaster, his characters' terrible vulnerability. It also suggests the dynamic nature of his style, the sense of a world beyond the frame, the compositions never final, subject to continual variation and modification. But equally striking, and equally typical, is the sudden cut to long-shot at the climactic moment, the action abruptly distanced, the foreground of the shot occupied by a large, decorative, bushy tree. The violence, and the hero's frenzied screams, are suddenly placed in a context of stillness and serenity. The opposition is central to Mizoguchi's art, and to his vision of life.

Or consider the shot, after Ohama's rape in *Ugetsu,* of her sandals (which have fallen off in the struggle) on the beach. It is in some ways a fairly close equivalent to those series of shots of landscapes or townscapes that punctuate Ozu's films, generally used as transitions from scene to scene or from one time of day to another having something of the function of establishing shots, but serving primarily as points of meditation—the action of the film suspended, the eye and mind given an emotionally neutral view (or, at least, a view not directly related to the immediate narrative) on which to rest for a moment. But herein lies an important difference: the shot of the sandals provides, certainly, a still point of meditation after the emotional and physical turmoil that have preceded it, yet it is by no means divorced from the action nor emotionally neutral. The stillness and emptiness of the shot emphasize, by contrast, the journey structure on which the film is built; its desolate effect arises from a complex of contextual implications, chief among which is our sense of her husband Tobei's responsibility for Ohama's fate. Where Ozu's "punctuating" shots are still points of pure contemplation, the shot of the sandals encourages in the spectator that precise balancing of contemplation and involvement characteristic of Mizoguchi.

The vivifying impulse in Mizoguchi's late films is towards wholeness and unity, and this expressed in stylistic detail as surely as in overall movement. It is an impulse that necessitates the maintenance of a certain emotional distance between artist and material, the purpose of which is not to deny or diminish the emotional intensity inherent in the action, but to place it in a wider context—a context both spatial and temporal. An event in a Mizoguchi film is never felt as isolated. We are not allowed to respond simply, with the immediate emotional reactions the event might provoke: we are encouraged to view the event within a cosmic perspective. If this sounds mystical (and we are perhaps too ready, in the west, to distrust mysticism, or confuse it with mere vagueness), it can be pinned down in the concrete detail of Mizoguchi's *mise-en-scène*. Consider two scenes where the emotional content is inherently very powerful: the kidnapping in *Sansho,* the mortal wounding of Miyagi in *Ugetsu*. Both can stand as representative of Mizoguchi's method. And though they are in some respects stylistically dissimilar, the underlying assumptions—about life, about values, about the function of art, about the relationship between the spectator and the action on the screen—are the same.

Sansho: Tamaki and her two children Zushio and Anju, on their way to join their exiled husband/father, are sheltered and fed by an elderly priestess who persuades Tamaki to continue the journey by boat. She in fact betrays them: Tamaki and the children's old nurse are carried off in the boat while the priestess and another boatman hold the children: the nurse is thrown overboard and drowns, the children break away and rush to the water's edge but are swiftly recaptured. Stylistically three aspects stand out: dynamic movement, whether of the camera or within the frame, communicating the intensity of the protagonists' struggle against separation: a preponderance of long-shots that places the violence, grief, and turbulence of the action in a context of natural tranquility—smooth water, still sky, motionless rushes, and bare tree: superb deep-focus images. At the beginning of the sequence the boatmen are introduced in an image dominated by the leafless, thorny tree left of screen but centered on the fire, beside which the men rouse to sinister alertness as they become aware of the family's approach. (The juxtaposition of fire and water is a unifying motif to which I shall return.)

The emotional distance implied by the use of long-shot has nothing of coolness or complacency. The extraordinary intensity with which the action is staged amply testifies to Mizoguchi's readiness to enter fully into his characters' anguish. The use of long-shot is, of course, inseparable from the use of deep focus. The effect is to hold the action at a distance while consistently emphasizing its reality. Nowhere in the cinema has the reality of physical space been used to more eloquent effect. Mizoguchi crosscuts between boat and shore, but never fragments, never destroys our sense of the unity of the action. From the boat,Tamaki in the foreground, we can see the children struggling to escape, straining towards her; from the shore, children in the foreground, Tamaki's frantic efforts to return are shown in crystal-clear long-shot. From shot to shot, the widening of the distance separating them is rendered with scrupulous precision, and the distance is always physically there on the screen, shore and boat in the same image. The style here implies the essential theme of the film, the tension between physical separation and spiritual unity, the family forcibly held apart yet united by Mizoguchi within the frame.

Ugetsu: Miyagi, trying to return home with her child, is attacked on a mountain path by three starving outcasts (perhaps deserters) who steal the rice-cakes she has been given. When she protests, one of them drives a spear into her. Her little boy still on her back, she staggers on, supporting herself on a stick. Here, there is no cutting: the scene is a classic example of what the French call the *plan-sequence,* the "sequence" organized within a single shot. But the preservation of spatial reality within the image, and the preservation of the spectator's distance from the action, are again crucial to the total effect.

For the great majority of directors, the temptation here would be to go for impact. One could invent a breakdown of the scene into twenty or so shots—close-ups of the men emerging from the hut, of Miyagi's frightened face, of the spear driven in, of the screaming, terrified child, of the woman in agony, of the men, showing their callous indifference—which could be immensely powerful in its force and directness. Mizoguchi's long take holds the spectator at a distance throughout, preserves the unity and continuity of the action, and preserves the sense of environment—of the action situated in a real world governed by the realities of time and space. We are not asked to respond simply and directly to the physical horror of a spear entering a woman's belly, but to an event existing in a context. The detachment with which the camera compels us to watch the action makes the emotion it evokes much less immediate and overwhelming, but also much finer and deeper: we are free to contemplate the scene's wider implications, to reflect on the events that have preceded it and its likely consequences.

The organization of the complex action over a large area within a single take is remarkable; one would call it virtuoso did not the word carry connotations of display, the technique here being self-effacing in the extreme. The staging has many of the features one thinks of as characteristically Mizoguchian. The camera position is slightly above the action, in the interests of clarity: from it, we can see not only the path and the hut, but down into the valley below. The path crosses the screen diagonally. As Miyagi walks along it, the child on her back, the men emerge from the sides of the screen, eventually surrounding her, and our minds are led back to the parallel scene of the rape of Ohama. The men steal the food, one of them wounds Miyagi, they disappear down the slope. Miyagi struggles to her feet and staggers on; the camera tracks with her, revealing the stick she takes to support herself, which lies at right angles to the path, hence making another diagonal to the frame—all the composition's main lines point outwards to the world beyond the screen. As Miyagi and the camera move on, we can see the men again in extreme long-shot in the valley, quarreling and fighting over the meager bits of food, their movements providing a strong if distant visual counterpoint to Miyagi's. The pain of the woman is placed in a context of universal disorder and suffering; our horror at the men's indifference is qualified by a sense of a world in which human beings starve to death and are degraded to an animal-like struggle for survival.

It is known that Mizoguchi had problems with *Ugetsu:* specifically, he was forced for box-office reasons to change his conception of the subplot. Originally, Tobei and Ohama were to have progressed, ironically, to great material prosperity and worldly fame as samurai and courtesan respectively; the ending would therefore have balanced worldly gain–spiritual loss (Tobei and Ohama) against worldly loss–spiritual gain (Genjuro and Miyagi). The film's actual ending provides a contrast that is much less sharp. In material terms, both men are back to square one, but Genjuro has developed spiritually while Tobei has merely accepted his lot. Genjuro and Miyagi achieve ideal union, though on opposite sides of the grave, while Tobei resigns himself guiltily to the aggressive domination of a very much alive Ohama. The resolution of the action works well enough, but the last-minute alterations in the scenario may be at least partly responsible for one's sense that the two plots are not very successfully integrated in the second half of the film.

A worse flaw seems to me the awkward and arbitrary introduction of the Buddhist priest who "sees" Genjuro's fate in his face, though it is not impossible that there is a cultural barrier here, a convention operating to which Japanese audiences would know how to respond. Relative to *Sansho*, *Ugetsu* must be judged structurally flawed, though it is still possible to value it above almost every other work in the cinema. Two elements in the film seem to me to demand attention if one is to offer some justification for so high an estimate: Mizoguchi's magical evocation of the supernatural in central scenes, and the reconciliation with reality, with "normal" human experience, towards which the whole film moves.

No filmmaker in my experience—not even Dreyer or Jacques Tourneur—has treated the supernatural with such delicacy and respect, with such subtle force of suggestion and so rigorous a refusal to sensationalize or vulgarize. Strikingly, the treatment involves the complete eschewal of all camera trickery and special effects: Mizoguchi refuses to tamper with the reality within the image, restricting his eerie effects to what decor and lighting can achieve and the camera record. Hence the suggestion that the Princess Wakasa's mansion exists in a world outside time is conveyed by our being shown it, unobtrusively and without comment, in three different conditions: first, derelict and decaying, the garden overgrown, the broken gate swinging on its hinges; second, magically restored and revivified by Genjuro's entry into it, the garden neat, the walls, windows, and panels as new, servant girls emerging with candle flames; third, as ruins, a few blackened sticks and struts (over which lie the kimonos Genjuro bought for Wakasa) rising out of apparently uncultivated grass.

The film's other great "supernatural" effect—the apparition of Miyagi to welcome her husband home—is even more remarkable. The camera is inside the house as Genjuro approaches, looks in at the window, opens the door, and enters. The room is quite bare and unkept. He walks across it hesitantly, calling Miyagi, and the camera pans left with him, excluding the right hand part of the room. He goes out through another door, left, and we see him through windows walking around outside, back to the front entrance. The camera accordingly moves back with him; but this time, as the rest of the room comes back within the frame, we see that its decor has been miraculously restored and that Miyagi is in the middle of it, cooking over a fire, awaiting Genjuro, who sees her as he re-enters, the camera now having returned to its original position. The *frisson* this moment excites is due largely to the simple technical fact that there has been no cut, no dissolve, no editing of any kind: the impossible has happened before our eyes.

The respect Mizoguchi accords the supernatural stylistically also involves rejecting any temptation to rationalize it. If we are led to find symbolic meaning in *Ugetsu*'s ghosts, it is by a process of suggestion that never destroys or undermines our sense of wonder. The "meaning" is suggested, I think, by the parallel my above description implies in both scenes: the house is, as it were, brought back to life by the man's entry into it. The scene with the ghost Miyagi clearly associates this with the restoration of marital and family union, but the ghosts of the central sequences, Wakasa and her nurse, were also motivated by the desire that Wakasa be fulfilled through marriage. The resemblances encourage us to connect the scenes in our minds, but the purpose of the parallel is clearly to make us aware of major oppositions. The Wakasa world outside time is associated with illusion, with the dream-fulfillment of unrealizable aspirations (the pottery vessels that Genjuro recognizes, somewhat hesitantly, as his own, were clearly never made by him in the "real" world), and ultimately with death the only condition wherein the desire to escape from the stresses and responsibilities of reality can be fulfilled. Mizoguchi creates its seductive beauty in a style that contrasts with that of the rest of the film while remaining recognizably Mizoguchian: the compositions are still built on diagonals, the camera still moves fluently, but the images look much more consciously and artfully composed, the camera moves away from one such beautiful composition precisely to frame another.

We are also, here, brought in much closer to the actors than elsewhere in the film: even in the culminating erotic scene on the lawn, there is a sense of oppressiveness. Wakasa urges Genjuro to stay with her and perfect his art—the art represented by the delicate objects she has presented as his creations, "art for art's sake," rarefied and out of touch with the outside reality where Miyagi suffers. At the end of the film Genjuro, mystically united with his dead wife, is turning a pot under her spiritual guidance, a pot as different from the *objets d'art* of the Wakasa world as it is from the crudely functional, mass-produced "commercial" vessels we saw Genjuro making and selling earlier. The new dedication he brings to the work comes across as the outcome of assimilated experience: the artisan has become an artist, in the full Mizoguchian sense—a sense defined by the style, structure, and significance of the late films. The fineness and depth of Mizoguchi's sensibility can be gauged from the way in which, having created for us the Wakasa dream-world with such richness of sensuous beauty, he can lead us to find greater beauty in Genjuro's ultimate reconciliation with the real world and the processes of life-in-time.

From *Ugetsu*'s last sequence I want to single out two shots in which the assimilative impulse of Mizoguchi's art finds perfect expression. One is the shot of Genjuro at Miyagi's grave. He asks why she had to die; her voice tells him softly that she is there beside him. The camera has already begun to track back, and as Miyagi speaks we see first the empty space beside Genjuro and then their son, kneeling at the graveside—the child in whom both parents are reunited, who represents what is perhaps the only immortality to which men should presume to aspire: immortality through continuity, and through what is transmitted. The second shot is the last of the film. In the background, Genjuro is tending his kiln, the pots so lovingly created, conceived as the joint work of man and wife, are baking in the foreground. Ohama gives the child a bowlful of the rice she has been cooking. He runs off to the right and the camera tracks with him to Miyagi's grave. He places the rice before the grave as if his mother were still alive and the camera cranes up away from him to reveal again the landscape with which the film opened, with two men in the distance at work in the fields.

Several factors contribute to making this one of the most poignantly beautiful last shots of any film. First, the continuity of camera movement that connects all the components of the scene, the pots baking, the child moving between father and mother, the underlying sense communicated of the triumph of the spirit over death, of the family mystically reconstituted and reunited, new life developing out of this reaffirmed unity. Second, the sense of continuity hinted at in the two laborers (for the film opened with Genjuro and Tobei leaving for the town), the sense of other lives being lived, similar to those whose progress we have watched, yet different, each unique. Third, the shot formally reverses the opening shot of the film which started on the same landscape and moved left and downwards to show Genjuro with his cart. This is not just a case of a satisfying formal symmetry. Mizoguchi having shown us Genjuro's story, turns us outward to the world, and the potentialities for experience it offers every individual. The total effect is to universalize the action, to suggest that the narrative we have watched unfold is at once unique and typical, that the path towards spiritual acceptance and assimilation is there for each man to tread in his own way.

I have hinted that in certain respects *Ugetsu* can be read as Mizoguchi's artistic testament. The three kinds of pottery with which Genjuro is associated, and more particularly his attitudes to them and the personal developments with which each is linked, are very suggestive from this viewpoint, especially in conjunction with the stylistic contrast I have noted within the film. Through his narrative, Mizoguchi rejects commercialism (the pursuit of easy money separated Genjuro from Miyagi) on the one hand, and ivory-tower aestheticism (the claustrophobic though alluring world of Wakasa) on the other, in favor of progress towards an art that will truly express the assimilated experience of life—art that resolves the dichotomy of "personal" and "impersonal" by growing out of experience yet commanding that experience through understanding and acceptance. *Sansho Dayu* made a year after *Ugetsu* can be regarded as the perfect equivalent for the pottery Genjuro is making at the end of the earlier film. The parallels between the two films are in some ways very close. If one regrets the absence from *Sansho* of the supernatural dimension that gives *Ugetsu* its uniquely haunting and suggestive quality, this is more than compensated for by the later film's undeniable superiority in structure and by the poetic density its structural perfection makes possible, for by structure here I wish to imply not only something that could be schematically worked out on paper but the delicate interrelationship of all the parts down to the smallest details.

The interrelationships are so intricate, so much the product of a supreme creative genius at its most alive (the aliveness a matter of the free intercourse between the conscious and the intuitive) that complete analysis seems neither possible nor desirable. It would quickly become unwieldy. Looking for some way into the film that will make it possible to suggest its nature without laborious over-explicitness, I fasten on its recurrent fire and water imagery, as an aspect conveniently limited yet clearly central. I use the word "imagery" (rather than "symbolism") advisedly. The most cursory consideration of the film should suggest at once the undeniable unifying significance of fire and water and the lack of any rigid schematic meaning attaching to them. Water is frequently associated with the women and with the concepts of patience and passive endurance, fire is often linked with violence and active cruelty.

But the dichotomy is by no means inflexible. The sea is associated naturally with danger ("Is the sea safe?" Tamaki asks the treacherous priestess the night before the kidnapping), separation (Tamaki helplessly calling to her children from the cliff on the island of Sado), and natural disaster (the tidal wave that has drowned great numbers of people at the end of the film). Mizoguchi never imposes symbolism on the action. Accordingly, the significance of the recurrent imagery is to be interpreted flexibly, in relation to the events with which it is linked. As the film progresses, it accumulates complex emotional overtones from the shifting juxtapositions until by the end the visual presence of the sea makes emotionally present for us all the past events with which fire and water have been associated, becoming one of the means by which Mizoguchi deepens and intensifies our response to the last scene as the point to which every impulse in the film has moved. At the beginning, mother and young children are walking beside a stream; at the end, mother and adult son are reunited in view of the sea.

The scene of Anju's suicide—visually, among the most exquisite (I don't mean the word pejoratively) things the cinema has given us, the visual beauty being the expression of spiritual depth—offers a convenient point of entry. It is a perfect example of Mizoguchi's ability to create images that are at once intrinsically beautiful and expressive and rich in accumulated resonances. His characteristic delicacy and reticence are there in the choice of long-shot and the sharply focussed tracery of foliage that part-frames and part-screens the girl's slow progress to the water. The cross-cutting between Anju and the old woman who has helped her brings in another recurrent and complexly treated motif of the film, the opposition between enclosure and openness, slavery and freedom: the old woman is standing in the gateway to the slaves' compound as Anju descends to the freedom of death.

That "freedom" is not entirely ironic. The tranquility of the setting and the sense of ceremony in Anju's gesture of obeisance to her old helper confer serenity upon her action. At first, in long-shot, the water looks like mist, into which Anju seems to merge, suggesting a gentle dissolution into the harmony of nature, the soul diffused into its native element. We may connect the stillness of the water with the name Anju was given in the compound: Shinobu, which means Patience. Anju's death is dignified—in Mizoguchian terms, or in the film's total context, made sacred—by its purpose. She sacrifices herself to facilitate Zushio's escape, and because she knows she would reveal his whereabouts under torture, and the aim of his escape is to reunite the dispersed family (and incidentally save the life of

Namiji, the sick slave-woman who was kind to them earlier because they reminded her of her own lost children; the ramifications of the family theme and its extension into loyalty-to-the-past reach everywhere in the film).

The water into which Anju disappears links her with her mother. Tamaki is consistently associated with water, from the image early in the film of her scooping it from the stream to drink (which inaugurates one of the flashbacks showing her unity with her husband) to the final reunion with Zushio by the sea. The image, inevitably, recalls the scene of the kidnapping (the dispersal of the family), but it also, less obviously, anticipates the scene of Zushio's visit (his escape successful) to the father's grave in Tsukushi, shot against a background of distant water. Our sense of interconnectedness is intensified by Mizoguchi's use of Tamaki's song ("Zushio, Anju, I long for you . . .") on the soundtrack as fitting accompaniment to the girl's suicide, half-ironic, profoundly poignant. The last shot of the scene sums up its emotional ambivalence, that characteristic fusion of the tragic and affirmative: the water has closed over the girl's head, but the ripples are still widening across the surface, Anju's sacrifice is both an end and a beginning.

The scene seems very close, in its economy, lucidity, and complexity, its extreme concreteness of imagery and its mysterious aura of suggestivity, to the spirit of the *haiku*. The essential difference is that a *haiku* exists in isolation, self-sufficient, while a detail in *Sansho* reverberates subtly through the whole structure. The final image of the water dissolves to the darkness around the temple where Zushio has sought refuge, a darkness almost immediately penetrated by the flaming torches of his pursuers. The progression is repeated later: from the scene of Zushio at Anju's memorial by the water, after the overthrow of Sansho, Mizoguchi takes us directly to the freedom celebrations of the released slaves, around a bonfire which eventually burns down Sansho's mansion.

The fire imagery is more consistent in significance than the water imagery, though the visual artist in Mizoguchi is always ready to seize on fire simply as the focal point for a composition. In general fire is associated with violence and evil: the boatmen-kidnappers are introduced huddled around a fire, and earlier our first view of the priestess has been introduced by a flame appearing disturbingly out of the darkness. In particular, fire is linked with Sansho, the principle of active cruelty and tyranny, as against Tamaki's endurance, Anju's patience, and the strength of memory and fidelity. Almost every scene in which he appears has a fire blazing; his habitual punishment for slaves is branding with a red-hot iron; his house is consumed by fire. Zushio's spiritual development in the central part of the film is from his brutalization under Sansho's dominance to his resolution to escape and reunite the family when a combination of circumstances recalls him to himself by making his sense of family real to him again. It can be traced from his acceptance of the duty of branding the old man who attempted to run away, to his decision to run away himself and take Namiji with him: in the shot where he lifts her to carry her off, water-drops suggesting tears of compassion are splashing from a spring at the left of the image.

One may comment here in passing on the consistent purity of Mizoguchi's treatment of violence on the screen, which avoids the opposite pitfalls of sadism and softening. The horror of the brandings is by no means diminished by the fact that in both cases they are just off screen. The scene in which the brothel-keepers cut Tamaki's Achilles tendon to prevent further attempts at escape is especially reticent visually (the act concealed behind trellis-work), yet extraordinarily powerful; like the other women present, we want to avert our gaze, despite the fact that nothing horrible is shown on screen. But the crucial point here is the treatment of Sansho's downfall. Mizoguchi refuses to indulge any vindictive desire we might feel to watch this monster meet a violent, messy death. He is simply denounced, bound, and sent into exile.

As in *Ugetsu,* the essential movement of *Sansho* is towards the assertion of spiritual triumph over time and space, towards that poignant fusion of affirmation and tragic loss. This movement, centered on the theme of family unity, is implicit in the film from the beginning, finding especially beautiful expression in the introductory flashbacks. Mizoguchi implies the continuing presentness of the past by dissolving from Zushio as adolescent to Zushio as child, running in the same direction from the camera. Even more beautiful is the linking of wife and husband across time: from Tamaki scooping water from the stream we are carried back to her husband making the same gesture as he raises a drinking vessel to his lips. Most beautiful of all is the sense that the memories are shared. The last of the flashbacks, showing the father's farewell, his gift of the symbolic statuette (the goddess of charity) to his son, and his passing on of precepts about the brotherhood of human beings, begins as Tamaki's memory, but at its close we are returned to Zushio, handling the statuette around his neck and repeating the precepts. What we took to be the mother's memory of the father proves to be simultaneously his: the spiritual communion of the family could scarcely be more subtly or more tellingly expressed.

The final sequence of *Sansho* draws together all the threads of the film: no scene is richer in accumulated resonances. Learning first of his father's, then of Anju's death, Zushio renounces the power he has achieved—which he has in any case jeopardized by his grand gesture of overthrowing Sansho and freeing the slaves—and sets off in search of Tamaki, the only other member of the family who may still be alive. Inquiring for her at the brothel where she was imprisoned, he learns that she was probably drowned in the tidal wave that has taken many lives. Nevertheless, he presses on around the cape. We see him pass along the cliff from which, earlier, Tamaki, lamed, called to her children across the sea. Tamaki's crying of her children's names echoes through the film. We heard it first when, on their way to join their father, the children gathered brushwood for the night's shelter. It was the enacted repetition of this childhood scene (when, as slaves, Zushio and Anju cut sticks to make a shelter for Namiji) that was crucial in recalling Zushio to himself after his Sansho-dominated lapse into brutalization—a scene where brother and sister heard, or seemed to hear, the mother's voice calling to them across space and time. The visual presence of the cliff brings with it all these associations. Zushio's progress along it is accompanied, on the soundtrack, by the melody of Tamaki's song, previously associated with Anju's suicide and now a reminder of the sacrifice that has made Zushio's search—perhaps a vain one—possible. The song, when they heard it sung by a young girl-slave from Sado in Sansho's compound, became the children's one intimation that their mother might be alive. Zushio passes on, crossing the little inlet which was the scene of Tamaki's attempted escape from the brothel, in her desperate effort to rejoin her children. It is low tide; Zushio questions an old man who is gathering together the seaweed deposited by the tidal wave. The old man is just telling him that Tamaki is certainly dead when her song, faint to the verge of inaudibility, drifts across in a frail, cracked voice. Zushio follows the sound, the camera cranes with him in a continuous movement that links the old man with the aged, lame, blind woman who is plaiting rushes outside a primitive hut. Though Zushio has difficulty in persuading her that he is truly her son—she has reached the point of preferring hopeless resignation to the further dashing of vain hopes—he and Tamaki are reunited.

Following a hint of George Kaplan's in the November issue, one may indeed compare *Sansho Dayu,* and especially this scene, with the late plays of Shakespeare: the recognition scene in *Pericles* offers the closest parallels, even down to the presence of the sea as appropriate setting, with its complex associations of separation, purification, endurance, eternity. It is a comparison in which *Sansho Dayu* doesn't suffer. The emotion generated is somewhat different—more desolate and stoical, though still intensely affirmative—but no less profound. Its force of affirmation is partly due to our sense of the spiritual presence of the father and Anju: in performing a noble, altruistic deed before renouncing temporal power, Zushio has indeed followed his father's path (as the early images of the film showed him doing literally), and Anju's death has contributed to the reunion of mother and son. Although two members of the family are dead and a third blind and decrepit, the sense of loss and waste is counterbalanced by that of achieved mystic unity, the past alive in the present, the dead living on in the survivors, the inherited values reaffirmed and validated. Those values are traditional in the best sense. Zushio has expressed his allegiance to his father's memory and transmitted precepts by performing a politically progressive action.

The last shot of the film closely parallels that of *Ugetsu*. From the embracing mother and son the camera cranes up, revealing sea and sky, a world opened up to us, and the old man still at work on the beach, laying the seaweed out to dry. The seaweed, a reminder of the tidal wave and its devastation, will be used as fertilizer, to foster new growth: the symbolism, quite unobtrusive, is profoundly satisfying as a summation of the film's progress, its implication of continuity and renewal partly compensating for the chief factor the ending lacks in relation to that of *Ugetsu*, the presence of a child. The rising camera movements that conclude both films communicate most movingly a sense of uplift, a sense of detached and serenely accepting perspective on life wholly lacking in sentimentality—a perspective that is implicit in Mizoguchi's style throughout.

The Samurai Film without Samurai
Joan Mellen

lthough it is set in the same period as Kurosawa's *Seven Samurai,* Mizoguchi's *Ugetsu* (*Ugetsu Monogatari,* 1953) contains not a single *bushi* hero. Nonetheless, it functions as a parable of that epoch of civil war and disarray that was the sixteenth century. *Ugetsu* is the story of a potter named Genjuro, who lusts after the great profits possible during wartime inflation. Obsessed with money, he leaves his wife and child to journey to the city. There he meets a demon, Lady Wakasa, who holds him in thrall in a mansion constructed in the style of the Heian era.

It is to the horror of war that the mansion of Lady Wakasa offers such marked contrast. In the scenes with Lady Wakasa, Mizoguchi's style changes. He uses long, smooth dollies around the courtyard and garden as Lady Wakasa flatters Genjuro with words he longs to hear: "Beauty is the goal of your craftsmanship. Your talent shouldn't be buried in a village." Yet, as magnificent as the cinematography is in these scenes, it is always in the service of a surface elegance, a superficiality that has nothing to do with true human worth. By its very beauty, the exquisite camera work depicting Genjuro's sojourn with Lady Wakasa poses an implicit contrast to the rough scenes of samurai brutality depicted in earlier sequences. The implied comparison at once passes judgment on Genjuro's "escape." The lovely photography itself, seen in the context of the film as a whole, forms a moral judgment on this man who has sacrificed all responsibility for the sake of passion, a lust Mizoguchi parallels with his avarice. The splendor of *Ugetsu* bespeaks evil. During the erotic bath shared by Genjuro and Lady Wakasa the camera dollies away from them, swiftly moving through the garden until we come upon the two languishing on a blanket in the grass, a shimmering lake beyond them. At the very moment Genjuro expresses complete satisfaction, the camera becomes uneasy. It travels away from them at the peak of their pleasure, in moral judgment of their selfish love. At another point the camera dollies toward us while Genjuro moves in the opposite direction, subtly conveying the discordance of his surrender. Mizoguchi deploys diagonal traveling shots in the scene where Genjuro searches the house for Lady Wakasa to express the same malaise. "I don't care if you are an evil spirit. I never imagined such pleasure existed," the potter exclaims, while the camera movement carries Mizoguchi's judgment that this phantom fulfillment is the very evocation of mindless individual surrender to a social order in disarray.

From *The Waves at Genji's Door: Japan Through Its Cinema* (New York: Pantheon, 1976), pp. 103–104. Copyright © 1976 by Pantheon.

Ugetsu
Audie Bock

The inspiration for the 1953 film that best expresses Mizoguchi's elegant lyricism was, as with the majority of his works, literary. Two stories from Akinari Ueda's 1776 collection of the supernatural, *Ugetsu Monogatari* (*Tales of the Rainy Moon*), and a Maupassant character study, *La Décoration* (*How He Got the Legion of Honor*), form the basis of a film that becomes completely Mizoguchi's own. The spirit of Maupassant emerges not only in the story of Tobei (Sakae Ozawa), the farmer who so aspires to the glories of samurai status that he neglects his wife, but in the vanity and greed of the main character, Genjuro the potter (Masayuki Mori). Mizoguchi's own recurrent themes appear in the fate of the two men's wives, Miyagi (Kinuyo Tanaka), who is murdered and becomes the spiritual guide of the reawakened Genjuro at the end, and the abandoned Ohama (Mitsuko Mito), who sinks to surviving by prostitution after being raped while searching for her husband. Throughout the film, a fidelity to the eeriness of Akinari resides in the tension between illusion and reality, while a transcendent environmental lyricism informs *Ugetsu* with a value beyond the pathos of human drama.

As in many of Mizoguchi's late films, including *Sansho the Bailiff, Princess Yang Kwei Fei, The Woman of the Rumor,* and *A Story from Chikamatsu, Ugetsu* takes a circular form, beginning and ending with a landscape that places all of the human events and emotions of the narrative in the subsuming context of nature. The camera travels from fields and woods to alight on the dwelling where Genjuro and his family are busying themselves with making pottery, and the narrative begins. Closing the film, the camera moves away from the little boy offering rice at Miyagi's grave near the same dwelling to rise again to the woods and fields, where a farmer can be seen at work in the distance. Like a classic Chinese ink painting with a tiny human figure dwarfed by towering mountains, the endings of these violent dramas restore a sense of proportion to human affairs: people are barely significant entities that live, work, love, suffer, and die within the greater immutable order. These enclosing moments of Zen-like space remove the viewer from the exhausting human passions and remind him of his role as spectator at a performance and as contemplator of life.

The presentation of the supernatural enhances the transcendental quality of the opening and closing shots. Mizoguchi's original impulse to do the film with surrealistic decor "à la Dali" was never realized, and instead he and Yoda brought

From *Japanese Film Directors* (Tokyo: Kodansha International, 1978), pp. 47–50. Copyright © 1976 by Kodansha International Ltd.

the supernatural into the narrative structure, using devices that resemble the classical Japanese Noh drama. The mist-enshrouded trip by boat across Lake Biwa, during which the protagonists encounter a dying boatman, was invented by Mizoguchi with a view to preparing the mysterious atmosphere that would dominate the whole central dream interlude of Genjuro's love affair with the phantom Lady Wakasa (Machiko Kyo). As in the structure of Noh, the entry into the supernatural is a journey, corresponding to the *jo* (introduction) section of a play. The central emotional event of the Noh, *ha* (destruction), is the protagonist's recollection or dream presented in stylized form, corresponding to Genjuro's entire experience with Wakasa, and her danced expression of her own feelings. In Noh the protagonist finally reveals his true identity, often as a ghost or demon, in the most dramatic *kyu* (fast) movement of the play. In *Ugetsu* Wakasa is gradually exposed as a vengeful ghost in the dangerous love affair, and Miyagi also proves to have only a spiritual presence at the end of the film. Together with these structural devices, however, lighting and camerawork lend a haunting air to *Ugetsu*.

The dream setting of Wakasa's mansion appears first as an isolated, dilapidated residence of the type sheltering neglected beauties in *The Tale of Genji,* the entrance choked by weeds and shrubbery, the walls cracked and crumbling. Genjuro sits waiting for the Lady to emerge from the inner depths of the house, and as a servant lights the oil lamps, the walls are transformed into well-kept opulence; the potter falls deeper under the unearthly spell. He drinks and converses with the lovely Wakasa, who flatters him for his humble pottery and completes his final enthrallment. When she sings and dances her love for Genjuro, coquettish looks embellishing her stately Noh-like movements, the voice of her dead father joins in with a muffled, rumbling recitation that seems to emanate from the warrior's helmet displayed in the room. We the audience by now accept these manifestations of the supernatural along with the spellbound potter because they are so subtle—no superimposed transparent phantoms, no dissolves and fades, no Dali-influenced decor calls attention to the otherworldliness of Genjuro's experience. All is kept in a supreme tension through affective lighting, sourceless sound, and realistic sets combined with the corporeality of the forms of Wakasa and her nurse. Even when Genjuro has had a Sanskrit incantation inscribed on his back by a Buddhist priest to thwart the demon's powers, it is only through gradual, shot-by-shot alterations in Kyo's makeup that her demonic nature is revealed. Then rather than make her disappear through photographic tricks, Mizoguchi moves the camera away from her, following Genjuro's frenzied sword slashing from behind as she and her maid retreat into the darkness of the mansion's interior and he falls exhausted into the garden.

An equally delicate cinematic assertion of the supernatural within the real carries though the remainder of the film and Genjuro's return to his country home. The camera follows him through the dark house, passing the cold hearth as he leaves the house through the back door. The camera pans back to the right along the interior wall, following the sound of his voice as he calls for Miyagi outside, and as the hearth comes into view a second time in the same shot, it burns brightly. Miyagi, whom the audience knows to be dead, sits cooking supper and welcomes Genjuro as he reappears at the front door. Everything in the scene looks perfectly real, but since we have seen it empty and dark and then fully inhabited within a single take of a few seconds, the effect is one of tremendous shock, much greater shock than if the transformation had been effected through a montage.

Characteristically for late Mizoguchi, the abandoned wife forgives immediately, refusing even to listen to apologies and excuses, in a departure from the original, where she demands to know all and then states, ". . . you should know that a woman could die of yearning, and a man can never know her agony." Miyagi's supernatural, forgiving presence remains even after her dawn disappearance in a further departure from the original story. In the last scenes Genjuro resumes his work at the wheel, and when Miyagi's voice assures him "Now at last you have become the man I wanted you to be," she speaks as the completely fulfilled woman. In a setup recalling one of the earliest shots in the film, Genjuro sits in profile at his wheel fashioning a pot; to the right is the pump that Miyagi had operated to drive the wheel; it stands still but the wheel spins. The fusion of the real and the supernatural culminates in this final scene, and we accept the life-in-death of Miyagi that exists in Genjuro's mind because of a cinematic presentation that is at once startling and unobtrusive.

Mizoguchi's sought-after lyrical ambience permeates the whole film through the treatment of the human drama in environmental long shot, but it assumes its greatest strength when it moves away from the human beings altogether. This occurs not only in the opening and closing coda of the film, but in the midst of Genjuro's delusion. The camera travels through the woods to fix on a medium long shot of Genjuro and Wakasa cavorting at a sumptuous outdoor hotspring bath. Wakasa coyly teases the enraptured Genjuro, and as she makes a movement to disrobe and join him in the water, the camera moves off again through the woods. As it travels it turns downward to the barren ripples of the ground, a dissolve occurs, the ground shifts slightly, and the camera momentarily edges past the circular grooves of a raked gravel Zen garden, rises, and shows the couple disporting themselves in a distant picnic on a lawn. Not only has time passed through the dissolve (in the original story Genjuro fails to return to his native village for seven years), but the viewer has passed through an unpeopled space that brings to mind emptiness and the transiency of human life. This moment of emptiness is of the sort that would be more frequently exploited by Mizoguchi's younger contemporary and friend, Yasujiro Ozu, but it is used for the same effect. Opposing Ozu's montage details of, for example, the famous stone and gravel Ryoanji Zen garden in the 1949 *Late Spring,* Mizoguchi skims his camera over the Zen symbol as part of the larger landscape of which the characters in the story are unaware. It is the spectator alone who feels the silent, transcendental reality between and beyond the drama of mortals on the screen, and *Ugetsu* becomes one of Mizoguchi's most profound statements on the delusions of ambition, vanity, eroticism, and the achievement of even so simple a goal as domestic tranquility. (In the original script, the would-be samurai Tobei never returns to his wife, but the production company would not allow such a bleak ending.) *Ugetsu* is the "chronicle of a dream disappointed, of a hope deceived," and the suggestion of the beyond in the lyricism of nature surrounding the tragic mortals in a small aesthetic redemption from their fate.

The Subject and Form of Traditional Theater Made into a Film—*Ugetsu*

Tadao Sato

The 1953 *Ugetsu Monogatari* is based on Akinari Ueda's 1776 bizarre short story of the same title. In the transformation to film, however, this classical tale has been fundamentally altered, similar to the case of *Saikaku Ichidai Onna (The Life of Oharu)*.

It was Mizoguchi himself who formulated the concept, and Yoshikata Yoda wrote the screenplay based on that design, following strict requests about many details. While this was going on, novelist and Daiei executive Matsutaro Kawaguchi published the story. At that time it was customary to have a well-known novelist take the story of a film being shot and turn it into a novel and publish it in a magazine for the purpose of advertising the film.

The original work consists of nine ghost or mystery stories. From these Mizoguchi chose "Asaji ga Yado" (The House Amid the Thickets) and "Jasei no In" (The Lust of the White Serpent). The original idea was to incorporate in these the theme from Maupassant's work, "La Décoration" (How He Got the Legion of Honor). However, Maupassant's story only provided a suggestion; the film did not borrow the story. . . . [Sato summarizes the Ueda stories, reprinted in this volume, pages 79–100.]

These two tales were combined into one in the drama. The character of the potter Genjuro is a combination of Katsuhiro of "Asaji ga Yado" and Toyoo of "Josei no In," and he is brought into contact with the ghosts of two women—his wife Miyagi, and the young beauty Wakasa whom he meets when he goes on a trip to sell pottery. Wakasa corresponds to Manago in "Jasei no In," but is changed into the ghost of a princess of the Kutsuki family destroyed by the wars.

In the plot of the film, the story about Tobei and Ohama is the part with a hint of Maupassant's "La Décoration." Maupassant's story is about a man who desperately wants to be decorated. His wife is having an affair with a member of parliament, and he comes to their house for a tryst. Unaware, the husband returns, discovers the decoration, which belongs to the member of parliament, and asks his wife about it. She tricks him by telling him he has received it secretly. He believes her and is pleasantly surprised. The theme of satirizing man's foolish desire for success is borrowed for the story of Tobei and Ohama, but because the story is completely different, there is almost no connection. By adding this, Mizoguchi

From *Mizoguchi Kenji no Sekai* (The World of Kenji Mizoguchi) (Tokyo: Tsukuma Shobo, 1982), pp. 104–204. Copyright © 1982 by Tadao Sato. Reprinted by permission. Translated by David O. Mills for this volume.

probably was trying to reiterate his life-long theme of criticizing the foolish man who attempts to succeed at the expense of a woman.

However, the production company Daiei strongly urged the incorporation of a happy ending in which Tobei, who is supposed to be the height of greedy ambition, happens to run into his wife, immediately has a change of heart, throws away the position he had risked his life to get, and returns to being a farmer. This scarcely believable outcome is the result of a compromise with the demands of the company, and was not Mizoguchi's own intent, according to Yoshikata Yoda's *Mizoguchi Kenji no Hito to Geijutsu* (Kenji Mizoguchi: His Life and Art).

Actually, as a result of this gentle resolution, the story of Tobei and Ohama lost its appeal completely. Nevertheless, what enabled the film *Ugetsu Monogatari* to be such a splendid work is the series of exquisite scenes showing encounters between Genjuro and the ghosts of the two women: the rare bewitching eroticism of Machiko Kyo who played Wakasa, linked to the mysterious beauty of the Kutsuki mansion in which she appears; the boundless gentleness of Kinuyo Tanaka who played Miyagi—more as a mother than as a wife. The ghosts of the two women stand out as especially attractive female images even among the large number of women Mizoguchi portrayed in his life.

However, why did Kenji Mizoguchi, considered one of those who established realism in *Naniwa Ereji* (*Osaka Elegy*) and *Gion no Shimai* (*Sisters of the Gion*), develop such a passion for describing ghosts in his later mature period? Of course, Mizoguchi did make the ghost story *Kyoren no Onna Shisho* (*The Passion of a Woman Teacher*) when he was young. And besides that, ghosts are one of the most important topics in Japan's traditional drama. Especially in No, the majority of the better works have a ghost meeting a traveler of this world and recounting his life and death with regret. Among Japan's film directors, Mizoguchi has studied traditional drama the most, so it is natural to think that his treatment of ghosts is his incorporation of the form and substance of traditional drama.

Actually, most of the attractive parts of *Ugetsu Monogatari* are the result of influence from No. First of all, for the above reason, his changing the snake apparition of "Jasei no In" into the ghost of a person has ties with story forms most familiar to No construction. During her life Wakasa was a noble princess who ought to have been blessed, but because she had to die without knowing love, that regret caused her to appear as a ghost and try to fall in love. She is wearing a No costume. Mizoguchi borrowed it specially from a No performer. Her makeup and facial expression were reminiscent of various No masks and the way she walked imitated a No performance. The Kutsuki mansion where she appears has a room at the end of a long corridor, and the view from the garden looks just like a No stage. That corridor in the No often becomes a mysterious passageway between this world and the other world, and it does in this movie too. When the lights carried by the maids shine one after another along the dark corridor and in the rooms, it produces a truly mysterious atmosphere.

Moreover, when Wakasa appears, the music includes a No flute—one with a resonance like a strong *kakegoe*.[1] Although the composer Fumio Hayasaka strongly pushed for western music, Mizoguchi demanded the No flute. In the music of Mizoguchi's earlier work, *The Life of Oharu,* he had Ichiro Saito try an experiment of liberally incorporating traditional Japanese instruments and Buddhist music into the western orchestra, and was successful in creating a unique sound. In *Ugetsu Monogatari,* he has Fumio Hayasaka blend No and western music more thoroughly. Not only is this a masterpiece of film music, but it also succeeds in opening a fascinating way to merge Japanese traditional music and western music; and Toru Takemitsu, who studied under Hayasaka, would later compose many fine compositions in this way.

When Wakasa begins to dance the *shimai,* a suit of armor displayed at one end of the room begins to sing No chant. It is the voice of a dead person from that other world. The Kutsuki mansion is completely transformed into the world of the No stage. That is a world filled with terror due to the appearance of the dead, and at the same time a world of ineffable elegance and sadness. Japanese ghost stories are different from ghost stories of the West and China in that the souls that wander this world unable to achieve Buddhahood are seen not only as frightful, but even more as pitiable, and the No expresses this best. The word *yugen,* which is often used to describe expression in the No, and which is very hard to explain, most likely refers to this kind of feeling, and *Ugetsu Monogatari* succeeds in capturing this *yugen* feeling in several moments. This achievement probably explains why this movie is the most famous of Mizoguchi's works in Western Europe.

The snake demon in the original story, "Jasei no In," is terribly frightening. It changes its form numerous times, chases the man it is after, and the monk who is to exorcise it is himself killed. In contrast, Wakasa is a far gentler, sadder ghost. This is because the most frightening segment in the second half of "Jasei no In," in which the snake Manago appears as Tomiko, is deleted. "Jasei no In" has a story sufficiently long to be made into a movie, and in fact a film with that title was made in 1921. However, Mizoguchi discarded this tale of horror's most frightening part, and replaced it with the completely unscary "Asaji ga Yado." Moreover, Miyagi in the original "Asaji ga Yado" is a ghost that appears desiring only to be reunited with her husband, whereas her counterpart in the movie is a mother with unbounded gentleness; she takes her son home even if it kills her, finds repose by entrusting him to her husband, and departs from this world. She is more a mother spirit than a ghost. In this way Mizoguchi's film approaches religion.

According to Kunio Yanagida's theory, ancestor worship is at the core of what Japanese believe. And in fact, we see a number of instances. For the most part, we belong to both Shinto and Buddhism. To believe in two religions at the same time may seem to be dishonest and irresponsible, but when you realize that the inter-

1. *Kakegoe* refers to a kind of intermittent shout to mark time.

section of the two beliefs is ancestor worship, you can understand that it is not necessarily so. What are called *Kami* in Shinto are the souls of distant ancestors of our tribe and race, and what we refer to as *Hotoke,* separate from Buddhist doctrine, usually means in essence the spirits of those of the household who have died.

The sense that the various souls of our near and distant ancestors are our guardian deities is the basis of our religious sentiments. Of course, that is not the totality of Japanese religion, but it is the core. Therefore, as is described in *Biruma no Tategoto* (*The Burmese Harp*), the Japanese think that the activity of gathering up the remains of comrades killed in the battlefield is the most religious act. Even more than thirty years after the end of World War II, Japanese still view the activity of collecting and returning the bones of a fallen soldier and giving them a burial as an ethnic duty. They believe that the dead cannot sleep in peace in a foreign country, and that the soul should become a guardian of the household and the descendants in a grave in their hometown. People in countries who were invaded by the Japanese army are uncomfortable when Japanese come back en masse to gather up the remains of those invaders who died, but the Japanese consider it such a sacred activity that they cannot understand why those people are uncomfortable. Therein lies the unique sentiment of Japanese religion.

The souls of the dead are frightening if they are carrying resentment, but under normal circumstances they are most dependable protectors of the living. Ghosts are usually the former, but in Japanese ghost tales, they often appear for the purpose of protecting families and children. Perhaps one of the most beautiful expressions of that role is Miyagi played by Kinuyo Tanaka.

Genjuro, escaping from the ghost of Wakasa, comes back to his home village. It is late at night, and his house is dilapidated and deserted. At first, when he comes into the house, there is no one there. But then, as the camera moves, it follows Genjuro entering the room, and the hearth which was shown earlier once again moves into the camera's range. Until a few moments ago there was no one there, but now a fire is burning and Miyagi is present. It is a strange scene. However, Genjuro does not think it particularly strange. Just as usual, she takes care of him, and he falls asleep. While her husband and son sleep, she takes care of all the household chores for them. Her expression is one of heartfelt contentment, and she moves quite slowly.

The wife who is in this scene has become a spirit of the dead, but she does not act like a ghost at all and welcomes her husband home with her usual kindness. This scene of the night is truly beautiful, and the warmth of Kinuyo Tanaka's performance is superb.

The next morning Genjuro is amazed to learn from the village headman that Miyagi has already died. In the last scene we see Tobei and Ohama working diligently near the home, and hear Miyagi's narration from off camera. It is as if the audience has become the ghost Miyagi and is observing them. As the camera moves up on a crane and follows the child running away from the house, Miyagi's grave rises up majestically, and the ending of the film shows the child praying in front of it. This movement of the camera to give the appearance of the grave rising up is excellent, and our surprise at the fact that last night's gently smiling Miyagi actually was a ghost is coupled with a feeling of solemnity. That solemnity comes, I believe, from showing the basic Japanese belief that the dead are watching over their loved ones from the other world not just simply as a concept or a fiction, but as something which is a tangible sensual reality. Surely, no other film shows the nature of Japanese beliefs this clearly and boldly. Akinari Ueda's original story, which was an adaptation of a Chinese novel, has become thoroughly Japanese through this transformation.

Filmography and Bibliography

Mizoguchi Filmography, 1923–1956

For a more comprehensive filmography with synopses, see Dudley Andrew and Paul Andrew, *Kenji Mizoguchi: A Guide to References and Resources* (Boston: G. K. Hall, 1981), pp. 43–162.

1923 *The Resurrection of Love (Ai ni Yomigaeru Hi)*
Screenplay by Osamu Wakayama. No extant prints, negative, or script

1923 *Hometown (Kokyo)*
Screenplay by Mizoguchi. No extant prints, negative, or script.

1923 *The Dream Path of Youth (Seishun no Yumeji)*
Screenplay by Mizoguchi, based on a novel by Suenori Osono. No extant prints, negative, or script.

1923 *City of Desire (Joen no Chimata)*
Screenplay by Mizoguchi. No extant prints, negative, or script.

1923 *Failure's Song Is Sad (Haizan no Uta wa Kanashi)*
Screenplay by Mizoguchi, based on a novel by Aimi Hata. No extant prints, negative, or script.

1923 *813: The Adventures of Arsène Lupin (813)*
Screenplay by Soichiro Tanaka, based on a novel by Maurice Leblanc. No extant prints, negative, or script.

1923 *Foggy Harbor (Kiri no Minato)*
Screenplay by Soichiro Tanaka, based on Eugene O'Neill's *Anna Christie*. No extant prints, negative, or script.

1923 *In the Ruins (Haikyo no Naka)*
Screenplay by Hanabishi Kawamura, based on an idea by Gando Kasuga. No extant prints, negative, or script.

1923 *The Night (Yoru)*
Original screenplay by Mizoguchi. No extant prints, negative, or script.

1923 *Blood and Soul (Chi to Rei)*
Screenplay by Mizoguchi, based on Ernst Hoffmann's *Das Fraülein von Scuderi*. No extant prints or negative.

1923 *The Song of the Mountain Pass (Toge no Uta)*
Screenplay by Mizoguchi, based on a play by Lady Gregory. No extant prints, negative, or script.

1924   *The Sad Idiot (Kanashiki Hakuchi)*
Screenplay by Tatsuro Takashima, based on an idea by Mizoguchi. No extant prints, negative, or script.

1924   *Death at Dawn (Akatsuki no Shi)*
Original screenplay by Matsuo Ito. No extant prints, negative, or script.

1924   *The Queen of Modern Times (Gendai no Jo-o)*
Original screenplay by Minoru Murata. No extant prints, negative, or script.

1924   *Women Are Strong (Josei wa Tsuyoshi)*
Screenplay by Nikkatsu Literature Division, inspired by a Shinpa play based on current events. No extant prints, negative, or script.

1924   *This Dusty World (Jin Kyo)*
Screenplay by Soichiro Tanaka, based on Kaoru Osanai's story adaptation of a play by Angel Gimera of Catalonia. No extant prints, negative, or script.

1924   *Turkeys in a Row (Shichimencho no Yukue)*
Screenplay by Shuichi Hatamoto, based on an American detective novel. No extant prints, negative, or script.

1924   *A Chronicle of May Rain (Samidare Zoshi)*
Screenplay by Koju Yokoyama, adapted from a Shinpa ghost play. No extant prints, negative, or script.

1924   *A Woman of Pleasure (Kanraku no Onna)*
Screenplay by Shuichi Hatamoto, based on an idea by Mizoguchi. No extant prints, negative, or script.

1924   *Queen of the Circus (Kyokubadan no Jo-o)*
Screenplay by Shuichi Hatamoto, based on a story by Tatsuro Takashima. No extant prints or negative.

1925   *No Money, No Fight (Musen Fusen)*
Screenplay by Shuichi Hatamoto, based on a comic strip by Ippei Okamoto. No extant prints, negative, or script.

1925   *Out of College (Gakuso o Idete)*
Screenplay by Kenji Mizoguchi, based on a story by Masanobu Nomura. No extant prints, negative, or script.

1925   *The Earth Smiles (Daichi wa Hohoemu)*
Screenplay by Shuichi Hatamoto, based on a story by Momosuke Yoshida. No extant prints, negative, or script.

1925   *The White Lily Laments (Shirayuri wa Nageku)*
Screenplay by Ryunoskue Shimizu, based on a story by John Galsworthy.

1925   *Shining in the Red Sunset (Akai Yuhi ni Terasarete)*
Screenplay by Shuichi Hatamoto, based on a story by Takeshi Nagasaki. No extant prints, negative, or script.

1925   *Street Sketches (Gaijo no Suketchi)*
Ominibus film by four directors. Original screenplay by "New Drama"

Department of Nikkatsu. No extant prints, negative, or script.

1925 *The Human Being (Ningen)*
Screenplay by Shuichi Hatamoto, based on a novel by Zentaro Suzuki.

1925 *The Song of Home (Furusato no Uta)*
Screenplay by Ryunosuke Shimizu, based on a story by Choji Matsui.

1925 *General Nogi and Kumasan (Nogi Taisho to Kumasan)*
Screenplay by Shuichi Hatamoto, based on an idea by Mizoguchi. No extant prints, negative, or script.

1926 *The Copper Coin King (Doka O)*
Screenplay by Kenji Mizoguchi, based on a mystery novel by Herman Landon. No extant prints, negative, or script.

1926 *A Paper Doll's Whisper of Spring (Kaminingyo Haru no Sasayaki)*
Original screenplay by Eizo Tanaka. No extant prints, negative; script extant.

1926 *My Fault (Shin Ono ga Tsumi)*
Screenplay by Shuichi Hatamoto, based on a Shinpa play by Yuho Kikuchi. No extant prints, negative, or script.

1926 *The Passion of a Woman Teacher (Kyoren no Onna Shisho)*
Screenplay by Matsutaro Kawaguchi, based on a ghost story by the storyteller Encho Sanyutei.

1926 *The Boy of the Sea (Kaikoku Danji)*
Screenplay by Akira Takeda and Masashi Kobayashi, based on an idea

by Kajiro Yamamoto. No extant prints, negative, or script.

1926 *Money (Kane)*
Screenplay by Akira Takeda and Shuichi Hatamoto, based on Marcel L'Herbier's *Feu Mathias Pascal*. No extant prints, negative, or script.

1927 *The Imperial Grace (Ko-on)*
Screenplay by Shuichi Hatamoto. No extant prints, negative, or script.

1927 *The Cuckoo (Jihi Shincho)*
Screenplay by Shuichi Hatamoto, based on a newspaper serial by Kan Kikuchi. No extant prints, negative, or script.

1928 *A Man's Life (Hito no Issho)*
Screenplay by Shuichi Hatamoto, based on a comic strip by Ippei Okamoto. No extant prints, negative, or script.

1928 *My Lovely Daughter (Musume Kawaiya)*
Screenplay by Shuichi Hatamoto, based on an idea by Mizoguchi.

1929 *Nihonbashi (Nihonbashi)*
Screenplay by Mizoguchi, based on a novel by Kyoka Izumi. No extant prints, negative, or script.

1929 *The Morning Sun Shines (Asahi wa Kagayaku)*
Screenplay by Chiio Kimura, based on a story offered by the Osaka Asahi newspaper. No extant prints, negative, or script.

1929 *Tokyo March (Tokyo Koshinkyoku)*
Screenplay by Chiio Kimura and Shuichi Hatamoto, based on a serial novel by Kan Kikuchi.

1929   *Metropolitan Symphony (Tokai Kokyogaku)*
Screenplay by Shuichi Hatamoto and Masashi Kobayashi, based on stories by Teppei Kataoka, Rokuro Asahara, Fusao Hayashi, and Saburo Okada. No extant prints, negative, or script.

1930   *Home Town (Furusato)*
Screenplay by Satoshi Kisaragi, Shuichi Hatamoto, and Masashi Kobayashi, based on an idea by Iwao Mori.

1930   *Mistress of a Foreigner (Tojin Okichi)*
Screenplay by Shuichi Hatamoto, based on a serial by Gisaburo Juichiya. No extant prints, negative, or script.

1931   *And Yet They Go (Shikamo Karera wa Yuku)*
Screenplay by Shuichi Hatamoto, based on a novel by Chiaki Shimomura. No extant prints, negative, or script.

1932   *The Man of the Moment (Toki no Ujigami)*
Screenplay by Shuichi Hatamoto and Masashi Kobayashi, based on a play by Kan Kikuchi. No extant prints, negative, or script.

1932   *The Dawn of Manchukuo and Mongolia (Manmo Kenkoku no Reimei)*
Screenplay by Shinko Kinema Scenario Division, based on a story by Otokichi Mikami and Sanjugo Naoki. No extant prints, negative, or script.

1933   *The Water Magician (Taki no Shiraito)*
Screenplay by Yasunaga Higashibojo, Shinji Masuda, and Kennosuke Tateoka, based on a Shinpa play by Kyoka Izumi.

1933   *Gion Festival (Gion Matsuri)*
Screenplay by Mizoguchi, based on a story by Matsutaro Kawaguchi. No extant prints, negative, or script.

1934   *The Jinpu Group (Jinpuren)*
Screenplay by Mizoguchi, based on a story by Gisaburo Juichiya. No extant prints, negative, or script.

1934   *The Mountain Pass of Love and Hate (Aizo Toge)*
Screenplay by Tatsunosuke Takashima and Matsutaro Kawaguchi, based on a story by Matsutaro Kawaguchi. No extant prints, negative, or script.

1935   *The Downfall of Osen (Orizuru Osen)*
Screenplay by Tatsunosuke Takashima, based on a short story by Kyoka Izumi.

1935   *Oyuki the Madonna (Maria no Oyuki)*
Screenplay by Matsutaro Kawaguchi, based on Guy de Maupassant's "Boule de Suif."

1935   *Poppy (Gubijinso)*
Screenplay by Daisuke Ito, based on a novel by Soseki Natsume.

1936   *Osaka Elegy (Naniwa Ereji)*
Screenplay by Yoshikata Yoda and Mizoguchi, based on a serial by Saburo Okada.

1936   *Sisters of the Gion (Gion no Shimai)*
Screenplay by Yoshikata Yoda and Mizoguchi, based on Alexander Kuprin's *The Pit*.

1937   *The Straits of Love and Hate (Aien Kyo)*
Screenplay by Yoshikata Yoda and Mizoguchi, based on a story adapted by Matsutaro Kawaguchi from Tolstoy's *Resurrection.*

1938   *The Song of the Camp (Roei no Uta)*
Screenplay by Shuichi Hatamoto, based on a battle song. No extant prints, negative, or script.

1938   *Ah, My Home Town (Aa Kokyo)*
Screenplay by Yoshikata Yoda, based on a story by Hideo Koide. No extant prints or negative; script extant.

1939   *The Story of the Last Chrysanthemum (Zangiku Monogatari)*
Screenplay by Yoshikata Yoda, based on a story by Shofu Muramatsu, adapted by Matsutaro Kawaguchi.

1940   *The Woman of Osaka (Naniwa Onna)*
Screenplay by Yoshikata Yoda, based on an idea by Mizoguchi. No extant prints, negative, or script.

1941   *The Life of an Actor (Geido Ichidai Otoko)*
Screenplay by Yoshikata Yoda, based on a story by Matsutaro Kawaguchi. No extant prints, negative, or script.

1941   *The Loyal 47 Ronin, I–II (Genroku Chishingura I–II)*
Screenplay by Kenichiro Hara and Yoshikata Yoda, based on a play by Seika Mayama.

1944   *Three Generations of Danjuro (Danjuro Sandai)*
Screenplay by Matsutaro Kawaguchi, based on a story by Naozo Kagayama. No extant prints, negative, or script.

1944   *Musashi Miyamoto (Miyamoto Musashi)*
Screenplay by Matsutaro Kawaguchi, based on a serial by Kan Kikuchi.

1945   *The Famous Sword Bijomaru (Meito Bijomaru)*
Original screenplay by Matsutaro Kawaguchi.

1945   *Victory Song (Hisshoka)*
Screenplay by Matsuo Kishi and Hiroshi Shimizu, based on a novel by Kei Moriyama. No extant prints, negative, or script.

1946   *The Victory of Women (Josei no Shori)*
Original screenplay by Kogo Noda and Kaneto Shindo.

1946   *Utamaro and His Five Women (Utamaro o Meguru Gonin no Onna)*
Screenplay by Yoshikata Yoda, based on a story by Kanji Kunieda.

1947   *The Love of Sumako the Actress (Joyu Sumako no Koi)*
Screenplay by Yoshikata Yoda, based on a play by Hideo Nagata.

1948   *Women of the Night (Yoru no Onnatachi)*
Screenplay by Yoshikata Yoda, based on a story by Eijiro Hisaita.

1949   *My Love Burns (Waga Koi wa Moenu)*
Screenplay by Yoshikata Yoda and Kaneto Shindo, based on an autobiography by Hideko Kageyama.

1950   *A Picture of Madame Yuki*
(*Yuki Fujin Ezu*)
Screenplay by Yoshikata Yoda and
Seiichi Funabashi, based on a novel
by Seiichi Funabashi.

1951   *Miss Oyu* (*Oyu-sama*)
Screenplay by on Yoshikata Yoda,
based on a novel by Junichiro
Tanizaki.

1951   *Lady Musashino* (*Musashino Fujin*)
Screenplay by Yoshikata Yoda, based
on a novel by Shohei Ooka.

1952   *The Life of Oharu* (*Saikaku Ichidai Onna*)
Screenplay by Yoshikata Yoda, based
on a novel by Saikaku Ihara.

1953   *Ugetsu* (*Ugetsu Monogatari*)
Screenplay by Matsutaro Kawaguchi
and Yoshikata Yoda, based on stories
by Akinari Ueda.

1953   *Gion Festival Music* (*Gion Bayashi*)
Screenplay by Yoshikata Yoda, based
on a magazine story by Matsutaro
Kawaguchi.

1954   *Sansho the Bailiff* (*Sansho Dayu*)
Screenplay by Fuji Yahiro and
Yoshikata Yoda, based on a story by
Ogai Mori.

1954   *The Woman of the Rumor*
(*Uwasa no Onna*)
Original screenplay by Yoshikata
Yoda and Masashige Narusawa.

1954   *Crucified Lovers* (*Chikamatsu Monogatari*)
Screenplay by Matsutaro Kawaguchi,
based on a play by Monzaemon
Chikamatsu.

1955   *The Princess Yang Kwei-fei*
(*Yokihi*)
Original screenplay by Matsutaro
Kawaguchi, T'ao Ch'in, Yoshikata
Yoda, and Masashige Narusawa.

1955   *New Tales of the Taira Clan*
(*Shin Heike Monogatari*)
Screenplay by Yoshikata Yoda,
Masashige Narusawa, and Hisakazu
Tsuji, based on a novel by Eiji
Yoshikawa.

1956   *Street of Shame* (*Akasen Chitai*)
Screenplay by Masashige Narusawa,
based on a story by Yoshiko Shibaki.

Selected Bibliography

For a comprehensive bibliography of materials on Mizoguchi in English, Japanese, and some European languages, see Dudley Andrew and Paul Andrew, *Kenji Mizoguchi: A Guide to References and Resources.* Boston: G. K. Hall, 1981.

Astruc, Alexandre. "Qu'est ce que la mis en scène?" (What Is Mise-en-Scène?). *Cahiers du Cinéma,* no. 100 (October 1959): 13–16.

Bazin, André. *Cinema 53 à travers le monde,* pp. 170–172. Paris: Editions du Cerf, 1954.

Bernardi, Joanne. *"Ugetsu Monogatari:* The Screenplay." M.A. thesis, Columbia University, 1984.

Bock, Audie. "Kenji Mizoguchi, 1898–1956." In *Japanese Film Directors.* Tokyo: Kodansha International, 1978.

Cohen, Robert. "Mizoguchi and Modernism: Structure, Culture, Point of View." *Sight and Sound* 47, no. 2 (Spring 1978): 110–118.

Gilson, Réné. *"Les Contes de la lune vague après la pluie."* (*Ugetsu*) *Cinéma 59,* no. 36 (May 1959): 98–100.

Izawa, Jun. "Mizoguchi Kenji no Sakufu" (Kenji Mizoguchi's Style). *Shinario* (October 1956): 28–29.

McDonald, Keiko. *Mizoguchi.* Boston: Twayne, 1984.

Martialy, Felix. "El Maestro Mizoguchi en 6 Criticas: *Ugetsu"* (The Master Mizoguchi in Six Critical Perspectives: *Ugetsu*). *Film Ideal* (15 January 1965): 44–45.

Mellen, Joan. *The Waves at Genji's Door: Japan Through Its Cinema.* New York: Pantheon, 1976.

Mesnil, Michel. *Mizoguchi Kenji.* Paris: Editions Seghers, 1965.

Moulet, Luc. *"Les Contes de la lune vague"* (*Ugetsu*). *Cahiers du Cinéma,* no. 95 (May 1959): 21–27.

Oba, Masatoshi et al. *Film Center: Mizoguchi Kenji Tokushu* (Special Issue on Kenji Mizoguchi). No. 48. Tokyo: Film Center, 1978.

Richie, Donald. "Kenji Mizoguchi." In *Cinema: A Critical Study,* vol. 2,

edited by Richard Roud. London:
Secker & Warburg, 1980.

———. *Japanese Cinema: Film Style
and National Character,* pp. 114–
120. Garden City, N.Y.: Anchor
Books, 1971.

Rhode, Eric. *"Ugetsu Monogatari."
Sight and Sound* 31, no. 2 (Spring
1961): 97–99.

Rohmer, Eric. *"Les Contes de la lune"*
(*Ugetsu*). *Art,* no. 715 (25 March
1959): 5.

Sarris, Andrew. *"Ugetsu:* A Medita-
tion on Mizoguchi." In *Favorite
Moviews: Critics' Choice,* edited by
Philip Nobile, pp. 61–69. New
York: Macmillan, 1973.

Sato, Tadao. *Mizoguchi Kenji no
Sekai* (The World of Kenji
Mizoguchi). Tokyo: Tsukuma
Shobo, 1982.

———. "Kenji Mizoguchi." in *Nihon
Eiga no Kyoshotachi* (Masters of
Japanese Film), pp. 81–89. Tokyo:
Gakuyo Shobo, 1979.

Shimizu, Chiyota. "Onna no Shunen
Mizoguchi no Shunen: *Ugetsu*

Monogatari no Setto o Tazunete"
(Women's Obsession and Mizoguchi's: A Visit to the Set for *Ugetsu*). *Kinema Jumpo,* no. 59 (March
1953): 26–28.

Sugiyama, Heiichi. "Mizoguchi
Kenji." In *Eizo Gengo to Eiga
Sakka* (Filmmakers and the Language of Image), pp. 122–
137. Tokyo: Kyugei Shuppan,
1978.

Toida, Michizo. "No to Mizoguchi no
Sekai" (No Drama and Mizoguchi's
World). *Kinema Jumpo,* no. 294 (15
September 1961): 67–68.

Ueno, Ichiro. *"Ugetsu Monogatari"*
(*Ugetsu*). *Kinema Jumpo,* no. 62
(15 April 1953): 54–55.

Wood, Robin. "Mizoguchi: The Ghost
Princess and the Seaweed
Gatherer." *Film Comment* 9, no. 2
(March-April 1973): 32–40.

Yoda, Yoshikata. *Mizoguchi Kenji no
Hito to Geijutsu* (Kenji Mizoguchi:
His Life and Art). Tokyo: Tabata
Shoten, 1964. Reprinted in 1970.